PIRATES
of the
WEST COUNTRY

PIRATES
of the
WEST COUNTRY

E.T. FOX

First published in 2007 by Tempus Publishing

Reprinted in 2013 by
The Histoy Press
The Mill, Brimscombe Port,
Stroud, Gloucestershire, GL5 2QG
www.thehistorypress.co.uk

British Library Cataloguing in Publication Data.
A catalogue record for this book is available from the British Library.

ISBN 978 0 7524 4377 5

Printed and bound in Great Britain

CONTENTS

	Acknowledgements	6
	Introduction	7
1	Medieval Origins	9
2	The Hell of the World	19
3	Venturers and Patriots	29
4	The Barbary Pirates	49
5	A New Age	59
6	The World Turned Upside Down	75
7	The Circumnavigators	85
8	The Pirate Round	105
9	The Golden Age	117
Appendix I	Western Men in Pirate Crews	135
Appendix II	Ballads of Western Pirates	139
Appendix III	Articles aboard the *Revenge*	147
	End Notes	149
	Bibliography	157

DEDICATION AND ACKNOWLEDGEMENTS

For Ma and Old Ged.

I would like to extend my sincerest thanks to all of the following who have helped in some way with the completion of this book: Jeremy Fox, Craig Long, Ken Kinkor, Anthony Malesic, Kass McGann, Terry and Anne-Marie Orchard of Brix Book, Simon Read, Duncan Spence, Mr R. Timmis and the aforementioned Ma and Old Ged.

INTRODUCTION

Pirates! The very word brings to mind images of sandy beaches, palm trees, buried treasure, tanned faces and clothes bleached by salt and the equatorial sun. But piracy is older than the golden age represented in the literature of Stevenson and Barrie, and more widespread than portrayed by Hollywood. Piracy has been called 'the oldest trade afloat', and though that is a little fanciful the origins of the 'sweet trade' are lost in antiquity. Julius Caesar himself was captured by pirates as a young man, and the famous Roman General Pompey set out ships against them. Similarly wherever merchants have sent ships upon the water to trade there have been pirates. Upon every ocean and sea pirates have been ready to plunder, to rob, and to murder for profit.

England has always been a nation of mariners, and the West Country has for centuries been one of the busiest parts of maritime England. It is natural therefore that a great many of the pirates of history have been English, and that a good proportion of those have been men of the West. In medieval times the South coast was the front line in the wars against our European enemies, and the centre of trade with our European allies. With the discovery of the New World and the expansion of maritime trade which went on to include the entire world the West Country was the gateway from England to the Atlantic. With all this trade it is unsurprising that piracy was popular in the West, and that the privateers (commerce raiders licensed by the crown to operate against enemy shipping) of the region should be so successful in time of war.

It is a little difficult to define exactly what constitutes a 'West Country Pirate'. Some great pirates of history were born in the West, perhaps sailed on ships from Bristol or Plymouth before becoming pirates, but their piracies were committed far away in the Caribbean or Indian Ocean. Other pirates were born elsewhere but used ports of the West Country as bases for their piracy. A few pirates, a small handful, were true men of the West Country, born in the West, operating from the West, and often captured and hanged in the West. For the purpose of this book I consider all of them to be West Country pirates.

I

MEDIEVAL ORIGINS

If it is difficult to define the origin of piracy then is it just as difficult to track down the first West Country pirates. The Vikings who raided the shores of the West in the so called 'Dark Ages' might be considered pirates, although they tended rather to indulge in raiding coastal settlements rather than piracy in the true sense of the word.

In 789 three Viking ships approached Portland. The local official took them for merchants and so they were able to land unopposed. The official was killed, and so began a long series of raids on England, the best known of which was probably the sacking of Lindisfarne in 793. If the Viking raids began in the late eighth century it was not until the early ninth century that what might be termed 'the Viking invasion' began. In 836 a Viking force of thirty-five ships landed at Carhampton in Somerset and defeated the Saxon army of King Egbert of Wessex. Two years later the *Anglo-*

Saxon Chronicles tell as that 'a great ship-force came to Cornwall'. The Vikings of this force united with the Britons of Cornwall and turned east against the Saxons of Wessex. Egbert met them at Hingston Down and this time was victorious.

The following years were littered with encounters between the 'ship companies' of the Vikings and the armies of the Wessex kings. In 843 the West-Saxons received a second defeat at Carhampton when the army of King Æthelwulf (Egbert's son), was defeated by a force of thirty-five 'ship companies'. Two years later the combined armies of Dorset and Somerset, under the command of Ealdormen Eanulf and Osric, and Bishop Ealhstan defeated a Viking force near Bridgewater. In 851 Ealdorman Ceorl defeated the Viking invaders at 'Wicgeanbeorg' with his Devon army. Later the same year the army of Wessex, led by Æthelwulf and his son Æthelbald, defeated a Viking force at 'Acled' and there 'made the greatest carnage of a heathen army that … [was] ever heard of'.

In 865 the Viking raids, bad enough in themselves, became full-scale invasion. A massive Viking force landed in Kent, not only to plunder and ravage England, but also to conquer it. By 871 most of England had fallen to the Vikings, but in that year Alfred the Great acceded to the throne of Wessex, which still held out against the invaders. In 875 Alfred put to sea with a force of ships and managed to defeat seven Viking ships in battle, one was captured and the rest fled. In the face of fleets of hundreds of ships such small victories against the pirates were of little significance. In 876 the Vikings were at Wareham, where Alfred succeeded in making a fragile peace with them, but the following year they moved on to Exeter, their cavalry overland and the rest by sea. Again Alfred ceded the town to the Vikings in exchange for promises of peace. In 878 Alfred scored a great victory over the Vikings at Ethandun, thought to be near Westbury in Wiltshire. Following their defeat some of the Viking leaders converted to Christianity and the war moved further East, leaving the West Country in relative peace.

Of the many Norman families which came over to this country with William the Conqueror few were as notorious and roguish as the de Marisco clan. In 1135 Henry II granted the island of Lundy in the Bristol Channel to Jourdan de Marisco, by all accounts a tempestuous and ambitious knight. The island is naturally almost impregnable. There is only one safe landing place where vessels may be brought in, the rest of the island is surrounded by cliffs and dangerous rocks, and all but the right wind prevent landings being made there at all. It is unclear which de Marisco began the fortifications of the island, but it is likely that they were begun shortly after the family took possession. In 1160 de Marisco was stripped of Lundy and the island was granted to the Order of the Knights Templar. De Marisco refused to be removed from the island and denied the Templars entry. Unable to enforce their possession the Templars were granted instead the rights to the revenue from de Marisco estates in Somerset until such time as he should surrender the island to them.

De Marisco evidently valued his possession of the island higher than the income from his other estates for the Templars were still claiming their revenue at least as late as 1202. It was one of Jourdan de Marisco's descendants however who made the name famous. Sir William de Marisco (sometime anglicised to William Marsh or Maurice) held the title and the island of Lundy in the first half of the thirteenth century, and used the island as a base from which he could terrorise and plunder shipping. By William's time the thick-walled Marisco Castle had been built to defend the island's harbour, and further round the coast the remains of a stone platform, believed to have been built for Marisco's catapults looks out to sea. It would have had to have been a formidable force indeed to have made an opposed landing on Lundy.

Despite a position at court and frequent favours from the king, William de Marisco seems to have been implicated in a murder in 1235, at which time he fled to Lundy. It is said that de Marisco's fleet operated north into the Irish Sea and into the Atlantic in the west. De Marisco realised the limited potential of robbing ships of their cargoes, and the difficulty of disposing of the loot for a profit, and so adopted the method of kidnapping merchants from their ships and holding them at Marisco Castle for ransom.

De Marisco had a personal enmity of Henry III, the reason for which is not clear but it was probably related to his expulsion from court. That the enmity ran deep is very clear however, for in 1238 de Marisco was instrumental in a plot to have the King assassinated in the Royal house at Woodstock. We are told that:

> a learned esquire, or rather a clerk, of the University of Oxford, bearing some malice toward the King, feigned himself mad and espying thereby the secret places of his house at Woodstock, where he then lay, upon a night by a window, he got into the King's bed-chamber and coming to the bed's side threw off the coverings, and with a knife struck diverse times into a pillow, supposing the King had been there but, as God would, that night the King lay in another chamber with the Queen.

When the plot failed Marisco found that he had made an enemy of the King and his supporters, but he was reasonably safe in his island stronghold. A small party of soldiers were able to land one night at the foot of one of the cliffs that make up most of Lundy's coast, and under cover of darkness climbed onto the island where they were met by one of de Marisco's prisoners. They were guided to Marisco Castle where the pirate and his supporters were surprised but put up a fierce fight. De Marisco and sixteen of his men were captured and taken to London. After being found guilty of treason for his part in the plot to kill Henry III de Marisco entered the history books as the first man to be hanged, drawn and quartered – a punishment invented specifically for de Marisco.

He was first tied to a wattle hurdle and dragged behind a horse from his prison to the place of his execution. He was then hanged by the neck in the same way as any other criminal, but was cut down before he lost consciousness. He was then stretched out, his genitals cut off, his stomach opened and his intestines and heart removed and burned in turn in front of him. Other organs were removed before his head was cut off and his body cut into quarters. The pieces were then treated to stop them rotting too quickly and were displayed at prominent points around the City of London.

As the medieval era progressed it became difficult to distinguish between pirates, merchants and the navy. Certainly some ships were owned by the crown, and these must be considered a navy of sorts, but for the most part the private merchant ships were relied on for the maritime defence of the nation. At the same time it is difficult to distinguish between the legitimate acts of privateers and downright piracy. The term 'privateer' was not yet known, and though ship owners and masters knew that they could attack and plunder enemy shipping with impunity it was often unclear what constituted 'enemy' shipping[1]. While the movers at court declared war and made peace it seems that the men at sea generally considered 'foreign' and 'enemy' to be synonymous with each other. The Hundred Years War with France (1338-1453) provided the pirates of the West Country with a 'golden age', an era when names and fortunes could be made by strong men with strong ships.

One of most successful of these men, John Hawley of Dartmouth, was utterly respectable. He was mayor of Dartmouth, was entrusted with the building of the castle and funded building work of St Saviour's church, in the chancel of which he is buried. In 1373 Geoffrey Chaucer visited Dartmouth and met Sir John Hawley, and it is generally believed that the character of the Shipman in *The Canterbury Tales* is based on this Devon pirate. Chaucer's Shipman is described as a wealthy merchant, which could be applied equally to Hawley, for he was one of the most successful plunderers of his day. In 1399 for example Hawley led an attack on a French fleet and captured thirty-four vessels, which were brought back to Dartmouth. 1,500 tuns of wine were captured and these were opened in the streets as all of Dartmouth celebrated the victory.

On Hawley's death in 1408 his positions were filled by his son, also John Hawley, who carried on the piratical traditions of his father. That medieval Dartmouth was a town full of pirates is shown by the number of complaints by foreign ambassadors about the seamen of the town. The pirates of Dartmouth were the foremost of their age in terms of audacity, and this is well illustrated by an incident which occurred in 1470. The Spanish ship *Marie* of Corunna lay at anchor in the harbour where she was visited by the curious townsfolk. The crew welcomed them aboard, gave them wine and healths were drunk, each to the other. Suddenly the Dartmouth folk rose up, threw the crew overboard and began to divide up the cargo amongst themselves. The master of the ship obtained an order from the Lord Admiral which allowed him to recover his ship and the cargo, but only just managed to escape Dartmouth alive.

It was probably because of the town's flagrant piracy that Dartmouth was selected as the target for a French landing force of around 2,000 men led by William du Châtel in 1404, the year after he led a raid against Poole. Hawley's improvements to the castle had been completed in around 1400, and work was going on across the river at Kingswear Castle. These defences forced du Châtel to remain off the coast for some days before finally abandoning his direct attempt on Dartmouth and making a landing at nearby Slapton in the hope of taking Dartmouth by land. Hawley however had not been idle while the French had remained off the coast and he was able to meet the French force with a small army made up of the local militia and levies, as well as armed townsmen and women. Hawley's forces held a strong position, and so complete was their victory at what became known as the Battle of Blackpool that almost the entire French force was killed or captured.

Another of the West Country pirates of this time whose name was known and feared by the coastal and seafaring population of Europe was the Poole man, Harry Pay. Legends about Harry Pay abound, obscuring the facts of his life, and it is often difficult to disentangle the two. What does seem certain is that by the opening years of the fifteenth century Harry Pay had established a reputation for his daring and cunning, and was much feared by both French and Spanish seamen. In 1404 the Welsh rebel Owain Glyndwr was leading his army through South Wales, supported by French ships in the Bristol Channel. As the French fleet lay anchored in support of Glyndwr's siege of Tenby an English fleet made up of Royal ships under Lord Berkeley and the pirate ships of Harry Pay, fell on them and inflicted heavy losses. Two years later a large force of French reinforcements for Glyndwr's army arrived off the Welsh coast and were met by the same English fleet of Berkeley and Pay. Once again the English ships inflicted a crushing defeat on the French. Later that year the French army was defeated, but Pay and Berkeley's victories had left the French with insufficient ships to evacuate their whole force.

Legend has it that following a bloody fight Pay was captured by the French off the coast of Normandy shortly afterwards. According to the legend Pay and his men were able to overpower their captors just moments before their execution and recapture their ship. Then, flying French colours, they proceeded up the Seine where they were able to plunder a number of unsuspecting French ships. Other legends have Harry Pay sacking the coast of Flanders, France, and Spain, carrying off the crucifix of the church of Santa Maria de Finisterre, and kidnapping important individuals for ransom.

For sheer continuity of piracy in the late medieval period the Cornish town of Fowey must rival, or even outstrip Dartmouth. So peaceful and pleasant now it was once the home of cut-throats and adventurers. Fowey had been a great seaport in the thirteenth and fourteenth centuries, but as the tin mining of Cornwall moved west, so did much of Fowey's trade and Truro was fast catching up as a commercial port. This slow but sure decline in trade coincided with an increase in the impact at sea. Although the Western pirates had proved themselves invaluable, Henry V had sought to suppress them, but at his death his successors did little to continue this work. So it was that the early fifteenth century saw Fowey declining as a centre of commerce, but growing as a centre of piracy.

The greatest of the early Fowey pirates was a man named Mark Mixtow, or Michaelstow. Mixtow had a fleet of three ships which he used, like Hawley and Pay, to plunder enemy shipping in the name of the king. In an age when almost all the armed ships at sea were taking liberties and assaulting neutral or friendly foreign vessels one must wonder how it came about that Mixtow was officially rebuked for his taking of a ship belonging to the Hanseatic League. Complaints about Mixtow were not infrequent, but he seems to have been no more prolific than some of his contemporaries who were hardly called to account.

Mark Mixtow was only one of many Fowey pirates of the fifteenth century. Thomas Bodulgate and Sir Hugh Courteney were well known as pirates in Cornwall, as were members of prominent local families such as the Arundells and Trevelyans, and the Lord Admiral of England kept a notorious pirate vessel named the *Mackerel* at Fowey. On one occasion in 1449 two ships owned by important local officials, including Sir Hugh Courteney, sailed up to Plymouth harbour and cut out a Spanish merchant ship riding there. At times the people of Fowey formed consortia to pay for pirate ships. The most notable of these share-held pirate ships was the *Barbara*, commanded by John Wilcock, which took fifteen prizes in seventeen days in 1469.

Although piracy had been widespread in the West Country throughout the early fifteenth century, the War of the Roses in the second half of that century distracted many of the more prominent nobles, merchants and citizens, and sea power played only a small part in the conflict. The legalised piracy which had accompanied the wars with France and had lent an air of semi-legitimacy to the pirates of the West, became diminished. Whereas in the first half of the fifteenth century acts of piracy and plunder were numerous, by the last quarter of the century it seems that piratical incidents were fewer, and those that did occur stand out more from the pages of history. At the end of the century a Genoese adventurer in the pay of Spain named Columbus set off west and discovered a new world, in England the Tudor age began, and men like Leonardo da Vinci began to think more scientifically. The medieval age was at an end and for the next few decades the seamen of the West Country were more concerned with exploiting the new age, building up their mercantile interests and seeing what could be had from the New World. Although piracy continued on a minor scale the massive increases in the size of the Navy of Henry VIII offered employment to adventurers. Not until the relative peace and stability of Elizabeth's reign was there really the scope for such large-scale piracy in the West Country as we have seen so far.

2

THE HELL OF THE WORLD

In the middle of Elizabeth I's reign the manors of East and West Lulworth were owned by Sir Richard Rogers of Bryanston, effectively making Lulworth Cove his own private harbour where pirate vessels could come and go as they pleased without fear of abuse. The local sergeant of the Admiralty Court, one Simon Lobley, was a member of Sir Richard's staff and both Rogers and Lobley turned a blind eye when a pirate vessel put into the cove and their crew was entertained by Sir Richard's tenants.

Sir Richard's activities rarely went further than that, but on occasion he would deal personally with pirates. Most notable was one occasion when Rogers was rowed out to the ship of Courte Higgenberte, a Dutch pirate who often worked alongside English pirates, to receive a chest of sugar and a tun of wine in exchange for immunity for himself and his ship. Rogers cut a mark in the mast of Higgenberte's ship as a mark of protection. Sir Richard's brother, Francis, however took a far more active part.

Wanted pirates were often entertained at Francis's own home, and he was known to have had a good wine cellar stocked up with stolen wine which he had exchanged with the pirates for bread, beer and other supplies. Francis often sent his own small vessels, well armed to patrol in the channel for likely looking prizes, until 1578 when he took a prize which more or less ended his career.

The ship in question was making her way up channel from Guernsey to London. Having boarded, Francis stripped the ship of all her cargo, which unfortunately for him included the Guernsey mail. A large part of the mail from Guernsey was made up of dispatches from the governor of that island to the Queen and her Privy Council. Naturally this last act brought Francis Rogers' activities to the attention of the Privy Council, who throughout Elizabeth's reign spent more time discussing piracy than any other topic. Francis was summoned to appear before the council to answer the charges brought against him, but dared not attend. Instead his brother Sir Richard travelled to London, where he was reprimanded by the council for bringing the law into disrepute, and was told to send his brother to answer the summons.

Francis never did answer the charges against him before the council, but the Rogers brothers careers in piracy were over. Since the authorities had had their attention drawn to the area something had to be done. Lord Howard of Bindon, nephew of Lord Howard of Effingham and Vice-Admiral of Dorset built a castle at East Lulworth and ended the pirates' use of the cove.

A little way along the coast from Lulworth is the Isle of Purbeck, most famous for the ruins of Corfe Castle, but in its time being the setting for the largest centre for piracy of the age, Studland Bay.

Pirates came from all over to trade their plunder at Studland, which by a quirk of English law lay outside the jurisdiction of the Admiralty. Pirates from the West Country, Wales, Ireland and

Holland all came to Studland to dispose of their loot. Provided the local officials were occasionally given gifts by the pirates the trade at Studland was quite open, plundered wares were displayed on the quayside, pirates wandered the town exchanging exotic luxuries for essential supplies. From time to time local officials engaged in trade themselves with the pirates, on one occasion for example Henry Morris, an official of the port of Poole exchanged powder and shot, intended for the defence of that town for fine wines from the Mediterranean. Local shop keepers exchanged their wares for African ivory and gold, wines, parrots, silks and spices. Merchants came from miles away to arrange purchase of shipments of goods at a very cheap price. So confident were the Studland pirates of their immunity that credit was frequently offered, the debts to be collected on the next visit.

Much of the bargaining for goods probably took place in the taverns of Studland, of which there were many. Pirates ashore would descend on the taverns for drink, women and gambling. Fights were far from uncommon and one tavern was described by a pirate as 'the hell of the world and he [the landlord, Will Mundy] the devil', not a far cry from 'the wickedest place on earth' as Port Royal, Jamaica would later be described. In the taverns also were men seeking a place on one of the ships. Out of work sailors and soldiers travelled from all over to Studland looking for employment.

One of the most colourful characters of Studland was a pirate named Clinton Atkinson, who went so far as to start civil proceedings in the Admiralty Court against a merchant who owed him £200. Atkinson not only appeared in the Admiralty Court himself to make his case, but was also allowed to leave to return to Dorset. When Atkinson was finally arrested in 1583 he was sent to the Tower of London to be interrogated by the judge of the Admiralty Court, Sir Julius Caesar. Despite giving away information concerning the distribution of stolen plunder in Dorset he could not escape the hangman's noose and before his death gave away to friends his 'velvet doublet with great gold buttons and his Venetian breeches laid with fresh gold lace.'

Another of the great men of Studland, and the first to be caught and executed there, was John Piers of Padstow, a man of the stuff of which fiction is made. Piers started his career picking off small vessels in the Bristol Channel between Padstow and Lundy, but worked his way up to become one of the greatest pirates of his age. His operations stretched from the eastern Channel to the Irish Sea, and his exploits include blockading Rye harbour in Sussex and plundering Royal ships in the Irish Sea carrying supplies and wages for the English army in Ireland. Whenever Piers returned to his home port of Padstow his mother could be seen waiting near the waterside. Mrs Piers was one of the most useful receivers of plunder as her reputation as a witch meant that few would go near her after dark. To the people of Padstow Piers was a hero, his activities brought money to the town and he was loved for it. When Sir Richard Grenville (he of the *Revenge* fame) was sent to Padstow to investigate Piers he could find nothing, so great and efficient was the support given to Piers and his mother. In 1581 Piers was taken, along with his crew at Studland, tried at Corfe Castle and hanged overlooking the bay.

The most brutal of the Studland pirates was undoubtedly Stephen Heynes, who was known to boast of his friendship with Sir Christopher Hatton, the courtier and patron of Drake's circumnavigation. Of all the officials who helped the pirates at this time Heynes was probably associated with the most helpful, not only did the customs collector invest in Heynes' voyages but he also stored Heynes' plunder in the Queen's customs house for him. Heynes' cruelty to captives was legendary, placing lighted tapers under their fingernails and even breaking their bones across his ship's capstan. On one occasion Heynes' own crew begged him to stop torturing the captain of a captured vessel, the *Salvator* of

Danzig, such was Heynes' cruelty that even his own battle-hardened band of cut-throats could not bear to watch.

A great friend of Heynes and probably the most successful of the pirates who frequented Studland was a Welshman by the name of John Callice. An illegitimate member of the Earl of Pembroke's family, Callice was sent to London when he was eleven to be apprenticed to Alderman Bounds, a haberdasher. Finding life as an apprentice not to his liking he ran away to sea like so many young men before and since and joined one of the Queen's ships under Sir William Winter. By 1574 Callice was master of his own ship, the *Cost-me-naught*, and for four years he sailed between the Irish Sea and the North Sea taking prize after prize and bringing their cargoes either to Studland or Cardiff. In his native South Wales he seemed immune, not least because his father in law was Sheriff of Glamorganshire.

In 1578 the Captain of the Isle of Wight, Edward Horsey captured Callice and his entire crew and sent them to the Tower of London. Dr David Lewis, an Admiralty Court judge and fellow Welshman interrogated Callice, and attempted to make an accurate record of the grand pirate's career. Callice offered a deal, in return for his pardon he would turn pirate hunter, 'I know their haunts, roads, creeks and maintainers so well, I can do more therein than if she [Queen Elizabeth] sent ships abroad and spent £20,000'. Friends intervened on his behalf and their offer of £500 for his release combined with his own offer secured his pardon. To settle his own vengeful scores he informed on a number of receivers in Wales, but soon turned back to piracy. In 1582 Callice captured the *Falcon* of Prestonpans, changed her name to the *Golden Challice* and made straight for Studland to sell her cargo, including two parcels of religious books which an Huguenot printer named Vautrollier bought for £40. The following year the authorities came down on Studland, sending in two Royal ships, which captured seventeen pirate vessels, including Atkinson's. Lacking a safe harbour in the

British Isles Callice sailed for the Mediterranean and began a long tradition of English pirates in that sea.

Further down the coast the wonderful natural anchorage of Torbay was a fertile ground for pirates, some of whom operated from nearby Dartmouth, or even from within the bay itself. In 1573 the Mayor of Dartmouth wrote to the Privy Council complaining of the outrages committed by a Captain Prideaux, who preyed upon shipping locally before repairing to his base in Torbay. At the same time a Captain Cole was ravaging ships in Torbay and taking them to his base in the Isle of Wight.

Of the Devon pirates of those years perhaps Captain Clarke was the most audacious. In 1575 Clarke and his two consort ships killed three sailors and a merchant when they attacked and ransacked the merchant vessel *James* while acting under a commission of dubious legality from a foreign power. Three years later Clarke calmly sailed into Dartmouth harbour and cut out a French merchant ship from the harbour, almost in direct view of the home of Sir John Gilbert, the Vice-Admiral of Devon, at Greenway. So inadequate were the provisions made that Clarke remained at the mouth of the river Dart for a whole day with his prize before disappearing over the horizon.

In Cornwall the activities of the pirates were largely controlled by the infamous Killigrew family. The head of the Killigrew family, Sir John, had the good fortune to own a piece of high ground at the entrance to Falmouth Harbour. When Henry VIII embarked on his project of fortifying the coats against French attack Killigrew's land at Pendennis was ideal for the siting of a small fort to defend Falmouth. Not only was Killigrew paid rent by the crown for the land, but he was also appointed Captain of the castle. During Elizabeth's reign the castle was enlarged, and so was the Killigrews' fortune and status. By the middle of the sixteenth century the Killigrews had built a new house at Arwennack, near Pendennis and had become *de facto* masters of Falmouth Harbour.

With associations stretching up the Channel and into the Irish Sea the Killigrews were one of the most powerful pirate families in history. Their ships had the freedom of English, Welsh, Irish and French ports, a fortune in stolen goods passed through the cellars of Arwennack House, and the Killigrews themselves seemed almost immune from retribution. For three generations successive John Killigrews involved themselves in piracy, each in their own way. The first Sir John, who was head of the family until 1567 took the most active part in piracy, fitting out ships and indulging openly in acts of piracy. His son, the second Sir John, was head of the family from 1567 until his death in 1584 and preferred a less extrovert role in the pirate network, mostly acting behind the scenes except in a few cases. The third John, who died in 1597, played an even smaller part and directed his energies towards the defence of Pendennis and Cornwall against the Spanish, though he is known to have turned a blind eye to pirates in Falmouth and even to have bribed others to do the same.

We must not imagine that the Killigrews were the only people of importance and power who connived at piracy on their doorstep. We have already seen how the Rogers of Bryanston suffered pirates to take refuge on their land, abetted by the sergeant of the local Admiralty Court, and how the pirates of Studland were able to arms themselves with ammunition intended for the defence of Poole Harbour. A few days before Captain Clarke was cutting out the French ship at Dartmouth, Gilbert Peppit, Sergeant of the Devon Admiralty Court was arrested at Exeter for his dealings with various Devon pirates, some of whom were arrested that same day. Peppitt maintained throughout that he was the innocent victim of a conspiracy by others who really were involved, and the Mayor of Exeter and the notable Cary family were implicated. It was Sir John Gilbert who complained loudest at the activities of Captain Clarke, but two years later seamen under the command of his brother Sir Humphrey were involved in the ransacking of ships in Dartmouth and Torbay. Throughout this period the fines exacted by the local Commissioners for Piracy on those found guilty of abetting pirates in some way or other were levelled on all strata of society, from tradesmen to mayors and the nobility.

That the piracy of the Killigrew family was not restricted to the heads of the house is clear, the wives of all three John Killigrews are known to have been involved to a greater or lesser extent[2]. The most flagrant of these Killigrew women was Elizabeth, wife of the first Sir John, and mother of the second Sir John. In 1582, when the second Sir John held the title, rumours reached Elizabeth Killigrew that a Spanish ship which had been forced into Falmouth by the weather had a fortune concealed aboard. A number of the servants at Arwennack, together with other men from nearby Penryn, were ferried out to the *Marie*, of 140 tons, in Sir John Killigrew's own pinnace and on Lady Killigrew's instructions. The *Marie* was rifled and then taken out to sea. Initial enquiries into the piracy were limited and little action was taken, not least because since 1577 the head of the Cornish Commission for Piracy had been Sir John Killigrew.

Eventually pressure was brought to bear and two of the Killigrew servants, Henry Kendall and John Hawkins, confessed to taking the *Marie*. They had been encouraged by Lady Killigrew, who had played a prominent part in parcelling out the loot from the raid. The pirates had not found the rumoured hoard of gold, so were grudgingly content with bolts of cloth and a number of leather chairs. The cloth and chairs were distributed amongst various members of the Killigrew family and their retainers. Lady Killigrew received four bolts of cloth, as did Kendall and Hawkins, two people who had supplied false alibis for the pirates received one bolt each. Sir John Killigrew's wife Mary, and her daughter-in-law Dorothy both received a bolt each, as did a number of the house servants. The six chairs were also divided between members of the Killigrew family. Old Lady Killigrew objected to having the chairs brought into the

house and so ordered them to be sealed in casks and buried in the
garden – possibly the only genuine incident of buried treasure in
the West Country.

In the cellars of Arwennack house must have been a fine collection of wines, which were probably offered to the many pirate
captains known to have been entertained there throughout the
second half of the sixteenth century. At least some of those wines
had been bought by Sir John in 1577 from the notorious pirate
Robert Hicks. Of all the pirate captains of the West Country in the
Tudor period Robert Hicks stands out as one of the most notable.

Hicks described himself as 'of Saltash', and was associated at
one time or another with most of the other pirates of note. He
was a very good friend of John Callice, and when the latter was
imprisoned awaiting trial in 1575 Hicks wrote to him, calling him
'brother', and offering his very shirt if it could help. Hicks operated
from Studland for a period, so would have known the other pirates
based there, there is some evidence that he later spent some time in
consort with Captain Clarke of Devon, and we have already seen
his association with the Killigrews. Hicks' final consort was the
Dutch pirate Courte Higgenbourte whose associates included the
Rogers of Bryanston and Lulworth.

Barely two months after the Privy Council wrote to Sir John
Killigrew to remind him that it was unlawful to buy wine from a
known pirate, they wrote to him again demanding that he investigate the seizure of the merchantman *Our Lady of Aransusia* by
Captain Hicks. The ship had been taken off the Spanish coast, and
when the owners complained about its loss Killigrew and his associates were ordered to search Helford and the surrounding area for
any sign of her.

Towards the end of that year Hicks was captured by George
Winter, one of the famous Winter family that included an admi-
ral and one of Francis Drake's subordinates. The previous Easter
Hicks and Callice had together captured a ship belonging to one

Johan Petersen of Denmark. Hicks had taken the ship and fitted it out to cruise in, and it was while using this vessel that he was captured. Hicks was taken to London where he was interrogated about his involvement with Callice, and in early 1578 was hanged at Wapping.

3

VENTURERS
AND PATRIOTS

The Elizabethan age is not chiefly remembered for its piratical characters, it is an age which belongs to the adventurers, explorers and privateer heroes[3]. Names like Sir Francis Drake, Sir Richard Grenville, and Sir John Hawkins are those we associate with the late sixteenth century. But the activities of those men, and others like them, were often very near the line between legitimate enterprise and piracy, and all too often on the wrong side of it. The most famous name of course is that of Sir Francis Drake. Queen Elizabeth called him 'my pirate', and despite his patriotism, religious fervour and unswerving loyalty to 'Good Queen Bess' it is difficult to argue with that summation.

Drake was born of Protestant parents in their farmhouse at Crowndale near Tavistock in around 1542. He was a cousin to the famous and prosperous Hawkins family, merchants and slavers of

Plymouth. In 1549 the people of Cornwall rebelled against the introduction of the *Protestant Prayer Book* and marched into Devon as far as Exeter. Drake's family fled the county and made their home at Chatham where Edmund Drake, Francis's father, made a living as a preacher to the fleet. Shortly afterwards Drake found employment aboard a leaky coaster with an aged master and so began his life at sea.

Drake's early career is inextricably linked with his kinsman Hawkins. In 1563 Drake joined the Hawkins concern and sailed as a junior officer on a trading voyage to France and Africa. For the next four years Drake sailed on a number of Hawkins voyages as an officer, and kept himself well clear of the piracy which was rife at that time. One incident which borders on piracy might be mentioned. In 1567 while Hawkins was waiting in Plymouth Sound to set off on a slaving voyage a Spanish flotilla entered the sound and failed to make the customary salutes to the Royal flag Hawkins was flying. Hawkins had his ships open fire on the Spaniards until the salutes were made, and though he was technically justified in doing so it naturally caused a great deal of bad feeling. Some days later a band of masked men boarded one of the Spanish galleys and set free the Protestant Flemish seamen who were chained to the oars. The Spanish Admiral complained and pointed the finger at Hawkins. Hawkins speculated that it was probably other Flemish seamen in the Spanish flotilla. Without evidence the matter was taken no further, but all concerned, including the Privy Council were well aware that the Devon men were to blame.

Shortly after this incident Hawkins set sail with his squadron on a voyage which would change young Drake's life. Hawkins and his squadron, in which Drake had charge of the tiny *Judith*, sailed first to Africa to capture black slaves, then crossed the Atlantic to sell them to Spanish colonists in the New World. Although Spanish colonies were forbidden to trade with merchants of any other nation, particularly the heretical English, Hawkins had already undertaken two similar voyages and the Spaniards had been only too pleased to deal with him on previous occasions.

By the time of this third voyage however King Phillip II of Spain had issued orders to prevent foreign interloping of the Spanish New World monopoly. At the first port of call in the New World, the island of Margarita, the tiny Spanish garrison was overawed by the guns of Hawkins' fleet (which had increased in size to around ten ships by now), and the English were able to trade for fresh meat and other supplies. Hawkins next sailed to Borburata, an important port on the mainland and the seat of the local governor. Here Hawkins could not rely on his strength to see him through so was forced to employ guile. In a letter he wrote to the governor he exclaimed that he had no intention of trading, as that was forbidden by the Spanish king, but if it were possible for him to simply sell some of his slaves he would be able to pay the soldiers in his fleet. The mention of soldiers and the twisting of Phillip's orders were the key elements of Hawkins' ploy. The governor however was away from the city on official business, and though the letter was sent on to him Hawkins was able to begin the sale of slaves while he waited for an answer.

From Borburata Hawkins set out for Rio de la Hacha, sending Drake ahead with two small ships to reconnoitre. On arrival at Rio de la Hacha Drake requested fresh drinking water, but here the Spanish were more determined and the 'treasurer' of the town, de Castellanos, responded by firing cannon at Drake's ships. Drake had visited Rio de la Hacha on one of his previous voyages and evidently knew the town well, for he was able to direct his gunners to fire two shot directly into the Treasurer's own house. When Hawkins arrived he demanded the right to sell slaves and again made inferences about the number of armed men in his squadron in the hope of scaring the treasurer. The Spaniard was not to be daunted however and instead of allowing Hawkins to trade he responded by strengthening the defences.

Hawkins landed his men and marched upon the town. There was the briefest of firefights in which two Englishmen were killed before the Spanish fled without casualty and Hawkins was able to enter the deserted town. With the town in his possession Hawkins was in a much stronger position to deal with de Castellanos and negotiations were opened. Hawkins was able to turn some of the Spaniards against the Treasurer and was led by some slaves to part of the wealth of the town. Over a barrel de Castellanos submitted and bought eighty slaves and a large amount of cloth from Hawkins.

Further up the coast at Santa Marta Hawkins made an agreement with the governor to put on a show of strength, thus 'forcing' the inhabitants to deal with him. The final port of call for the Englishmen was to have been Cartagena. At that city they found the inhabitants, garrison, and authorities so determined not to allow trade, and so well fortified to defend their resolution, that after briefly testing the defences Hawkins decided to set sail for home. By leaving at that time Hawkins hoped to avoid the period of bad storms which was expected to descend on the Caribbean at any time. However, the English had already left it too late and three weeks after leaving Cartagena, while off the coast of Florida the squadron was engulfed in a terrible storm which lasted for four days. The ships, and in particular Hawkins' flagship, the *Jesus of Lübeck*, were so badly battered that they were forced to run for the major port of San Juan de Ulua. The annual Spanish treasure flota was expected to arrive at the port at the same time to collect the produce of the Mexican mines, and for Hawkins it was a grave risk that they would be caught in harbour by the powerful Spanish squadron. He had little choice however and in mid-September 1568 the English squadron anchored in the harbour under false colours, captured the batteries defending the port and set about their repairs. Hawkins immediately set about showing that his intentions were friendly. He at once sent a letter to the Spanish authorities in Mexico stating that he had been forced into San

Juan de Ulua by adverse weather and that he intended to pay in full for any supplies he received.

The following day however there appeared outside the harbour thirteen heavily armed Spanish galleons, the treasure fleet whose arrival Hawkins had so feared. Both commanders faced a diplomatic and military quandary. Hawkins on the one hand could not deny the Spanish entry into their own harbour without causing a diplomatic incident of the greatest seriousness, but neither could he adequately defend himself or his ships if he let the Spaniards into the harbour. For the Spanish commander, Don Martin Enriquez the problem was just as thorny. He could not possibly wait outside the harbour, for the weather was against him and he risked his ship every day he did so. Neither could he force his way into the harbour for the same reason that Hawkins could not keep him out by force, but furthermore he was forbidden to enter into negotiations with the heretical English. In the end he resolved upon a compromise. He would negotiate a peaceful agreement with the English whereby he would enter the harbour, but would not interfere with the English fleet, and then, to satisfy his obligation to King Phillip, he would break the agreement.

So it was that three days after their arrival the Spanish fleet entered the harbour and moored together, a little away from where the English fleet had moored together. Three days later the English observed the Spanish shifting guns about and having the general appearance of getting ready for battle. In the late afternoon the Spanish launched their attack. A large number of English seamen were ashore at the time, and as they retreated towards their ships they were cut off and slaughtered. One of the Spanish ships drifted against the *Judith* in an attempt to attack her, but Drake had been too cautious and she was quickly pulled out of harm's way. The *Jesus* and the *Minion* also managed to escape, but the Spanish had recaptured their land battery and now opened fire on the escaping vessels. All of the masts of the *Jesus* were shot through, so with no hope of sailing her away, and indeed little hope of any ship escaping, the *Jesus* was used as a shield for the *Minion* to get past the guns on shore. Drake in the *Judith* made straight for England while Hawkins in the *Minion* sailed first to the Mexican coast where 100 men asked to be put ashore. Only twenty men of the *Minion* survived the journey home, and the treachery of the Spanish was deeply ingrained on Drake's mind forever.

In the same year that Hawkins and young Drake returned to England another West Country pirate by the name of Sir Thomas Stucley was leaving. It was widely rumoured that Stucley was the illegitimate son of Henry VIII, but he spent his childhood at Affleton, near Ilfracombe, in the home of Sir Hugh Stucley. At a fairly young age he entered the service of the Duke of Somerset, guardian of the young King Edward VI, but when Somerset was outmanoeuvred politically and removed from power Stucley fled the country in 1551. The following year Stucley was given a letter of recommendation to King Edward by King Henri II of France, and immediately proved his loyalty by revealing plans of a French invasion. For the next few years Stucley was driven by poverty to join the household of the Duke of Savoy as a soldier of fortune, which service he left in 1558 to pursue a career at sea.

In 1563 Stucley was once more in England where he joined with the Huguenot privateer Jean Ribaut on an expedition to Florida and the Carribean. Nominally the expedition was one of colonisation, and indeed Ribaut oversaw the building of Fort Caroline, one of the earliest French settlements in the New World, but the two adventurers took the opportunity to take some prizes by piracy. In 1565 Stucley was arrested for his activities with Ribaut. Although his trial was a mere formality and there was no question of punishment, Queen Elizabeth felt the need to distance her self officially and publicly from the rogue whose exploits she had helped finance.

After a short time serving with the English army in Ireland Stucley returned to the continent where he was received first at the

French and then at the Spanish courts. In 1571 Stucley had command of three galleys in Don John of Austria's fleet at the Battle of Lepanto, one of the greatest sea battles fought to that date or since. The following year Stucley was once more in Spain, this time offering to use a fleet of twenty ships to hold the English Channel against the English. Phillip II of Spain prevaricated endlessly so a frustrated Stucley set off to seek backing from the Pope. In 1578 a Papal force under Stucley's command set off to invade Ireland. Since more ships, soldiers and supplies were required Stucley put his force into Lisbon where he was distracted by the Portuguese King Sebastian's plans for an attack on Morocco. At the Battle of Alcazar Stucley, the self styled 'Marquis of Ireland', was killed.

Whether Hawkins' voyage of 1567-9 had been piratical is debatable, but there is no question that Drake's reaction to the battle of San Juan de Ulua was to embark on a fifteen-year career of outright piracy. Piracy inspired by righteous and religious indignation perhaps, but piracy nonetheless.

In 1570 Drake set out on the first of his raids against the Isthmus of Panama. Although pirates of other nations had been active in that area for some years Drake was probably the first Englishman to embark on purely piratical expeditions against the Spanish Main. Little is known about Drake's first voyage of plunder against the Spanish Main: he sailed in his own ship, the *Swan* of only twenty-five tons, and although he doubtless missed no opportunity for plunder the voyage seems to have been one of intelligence gathering and reconnaissance. Most importantly Drake made contact with escaped slaves called Cimaroons, and discovered a small natural harbour which he named Port Pheasant and at which he buried his excess supplies in anticipation of returning. The harbour itself was said to be ideal, it was deep enough and broad enough to house a small squadron, the narrow entrance meant that it was protected from the wind in any direction and was partially concealed, best of all nobody but Drake and his crew knew of it.

In May 1572 Drake set sail from Plymouth harbour with two vessels, the *Pascoe* of seventy tons and his own *Swan*, which was commanded by his brother John. They were heading once more for the Isthmus of Panama on a voyage which would make Francis' fortune and reputation. Forty-nine days later the two ships sailed through the narrow entrance of Port Pheasant. They had not been spotted by any other ships, they had taken on fresh water and caught fresh fish, and Port Pheasant itself has been described as an 'Elysian harbour' and 'Eden'. For the seventy-three young English men, all of whom except one were aged under thirty, it must indeed have seemed that their luck was in. However, as the ships entered their anchorage a slowly rising pillar of smoke was spotted on the shore. Drake went away in one of the boats to investigate and stepping ashore found a lead plate nailed to a tree:

> Captain Drake, if you fortune to come to this port make haste away, for the Spaniards which you had with you here last year have bewrayed the place and taken away all that you left here. I departed from hence this present 7 of July 1572. You very loving friend, John Garret.

Garret was another Devon seaman with whom Drake was acquainted. Evidently Drake's secret harbour was not as secret as he had hoped. Undaunted by the loss of his spare supplies and by Garret's warning Drake decided to fortify Port Pheasant. There was no Spanish garrison within 100 miles and they could hardly know that Drake was on the coast anyway. He also had his men assemble three pinnaces, small light vessels which had been brought out from England in the holds of the other vessels and which could operate in all but the shallowest water. While this work was going on Drake suffered another blow when a second English ship commanded by Captain James Raunse arrived at Port Pheasant. Clearly the secret base he had discovered was becoming common knowledge amongst English seamen.

Making the best of a bad situation Drake suggested that some of Raunse's men join his own for a raid on the treasure town of Nombre de Dios. Nombre de Dios was the town on the Spanish Main to which much of the gold and silver taken from the mines was transported, and where it was loaded onto the treasure galleons for removal to Spain. With only around sixty men Drake landed in a secluded bay just along the coast from the town in the small hours of the morning. Drake knew the streets of the town, for he had visited it on his previous voyage and explored the avenues and alleys in disguise. A battery of guns overlooked the bay in which they had landed, but only one gunner stood watch there and he quickly ran off. Drake led his men to the main battery which had been built overlooking the town, only to find that the building work was incomplete and that no guns had been sent there yet. Here the English divided into two divisions. John Drake and John Oxenham, one of the other officers, set off with eighteen men to enter the main market place by circling behind the Treasure House, while Francis Drake led the other forty men up the main street with drums and trumpets proclaiming their presence. Most of the inhabitants of the town had fled without even knowing what the threat to them was, but fourteen or fifteen armed themselves with muskets and returned to the market square where they met Drake's main party. A volley was fired in which the trumpeter was killed and Drake himself was shot through the leg. The English returned fire with a volley of muskets and arrows then fell upon the Spaniards with swords and axes. The Spaniards put up a fierce fight until the party led by John Drake and John Oxenham reached the market place and attacked their rear. The Spanish fled and Drake led the English to the governor's house, in which was stored the silver waiting for transport to Spain.

As the Spanish inhabitants began to realise the tiny size of the force from which they had fled they began to file back into the town, so Drake called his men away from the silver and to their arms. Word reached them that their pinnaces were in danger, and time was of the essence. At about this time a flash storm, not uncommon in the tropics, opened the heavens over Nombre de Dios, soaking the powder and bowstrings of the English raiders. Drake's men began to murmur of fleeing the town, but Drake responded in a typically memorable way – 'I have brought you to the treasure house of the World. If you leave without it you may henceforth blame nobody but yourselves' he told them. As soon as the storm ended John Drake and Oxenham were sent to the water's edge to break into the treasure house where the gold was stored, while he led the main party to hold the market place once more against the Spaniards. At this moment disaster struck'.

Drake had not revealed his leg wound to anyone but now he fainted from it and his men noticed that he was leaving blood-stained footprints in the sand. His men bandaged his leg and carried him to the pinnaces, and the entire English force followed and put to sea away from Nombre de Dios.

When they managed to rendezvous with their ships and their comrades Captain Raunse announced his intention to leave Drake's company. The Spanish were now alerted to their presence on the coast, he had one or two prizes of his own and he would sail for England. For several months Drake remained in the Caribbean carrying out small scale raids on towns and plundering Spanish ships. During this time Drake's brothers John and Joseph both died, John from wounds he received boarding a Spanish galleon and Joseph from the yellow fever which decimated Drake's force. In early 1573 Drake's Cimarroon allies told him that the mule train which carried Spanish gold and silver from Panama to the port of Venta Cruces was shortly to set off through the jungle along the 'Camino Real', the Royal Road.

There was more than one party of mules. The first coming East from Panama carried only silks and other commodities – valuable in themselves, but worthless compared to the gold and silver carried by the second train. Coming in the opposite direction was another mule train carrying nothing but supplies from Spain to Panama. It was essential that Drake's men and his Cimaroon allies allow the first mule train, and the one heading to Panama, to pass them before they attacked the second train carrying the gold and silver. While everyone was in position, ready for the raid which should have made them wealthy men, one of Drake's men who had been drinking heavily stood up to attack the wrong mule train, that carrying supplies to Panama. A Cimaroon quickly pounced on him and dragged him into the undergrowth but he had been spotted and the Spanish were warned of their presence. Once more Drake had to return to his ships empty handed. The voyage into the jungle was not a complete waste however. The Cimaroons took Drake and his men to the watershed of the Isthmus, from which could be seen the Pacific Ocean. Both Drake and Oxenham swore that they would one day sail upon it.

Some time later Drake met up with the noted French privateer and cartographer Guillaume le Têtu. With le Têtu's assistance Drake proposed a raid on another mule train carrying silver to Nombre de Dios. This time the attack was more successful and the raiders acquired more silver than they could carry. Each man took as much silver as he could manage and the rest was buried. The wounded, included le Têtu were left with the buried silver while the rest went off to the shore. Here they had intended to load up their pinnaces then return for the wounded and the rest of their loot, but the pinnaces had been forced out to sea, by the arrival of a Spanish squadron. Undaunted Drake built a raft and with four men set off in search of the pinnaces. Eventually they met and returned to where Drake had left his men. They loaded the silver aboard and set off to rescue their wounded and retrieve the rest of their haul. Unfortunately while Drake had been searching for the pinnaces the Spanish had found the wounded men. Le Têtu and the others were all killed and the treasure was dug up.

Satisfied at last that the voyage was showing a profit Drake decided to return home. The *Swan* had been deliberately scuttled some months previously, and now it was decided that the *Pascoe* was not in a fit state to make a journey across the Atlantic, so a Spanish ship was captured and the treasure was transferred into her. Drake broke up the little pinnaces which had served him so well and presented the iron fittings from them to the Cimaroons to turn into arrow heads. In April 1573 Drake anchored in Plymouth harbour and his place in history was assured.

For the next few years Drake spent his time serving the Crown in European waters, he was probably involved in the naval part of English operations in Ireland. His comrade from their voyage to the Caribbean, John Oxenham, however was busy fitting out an expedition to return to the Caribbean, to capitalise on the experience and knowledge of the area gained in nearly two years of piracy there.

In April 1576 Oxenham set sail with a ship of around 140 tons and a crew of seventy men. His intention was to imitate the attacks on the mule trains which he had undertaken with Drake four years previously. When he reached the Spanish Main however, and was able to consult with the Cimaroons, he discovered that since Drake's attacks the mule trains had been guarded by Spanish soldiers. Lacking a force strong enough to oppose the Spanish soldiers Oxenham laid new plans, and resolved to fulfil the vow he had made to sail on the Pacific.

Having learned the use of smaller vessels from his experiences with Drake, Oxenham had included two prefabricated pinnaces in the supplies for his expedition. Near Nombre de Dios he beached his ship, and unloaded all the cannons from her. The ship he covered with branches and the guns were buried. He and his men, guided by Cimaroons, then set out across the Isthmus of Panama. After about 35 miles the pirates reached the bank of a navigable river where they built a pinnace. A Spanish account of Oxenham's expedition has it that he built this pinnace out of wood cut from the surrounding jungle, but it seems more likely that it was one of the two he had brought from England. Once the pinnace was built they sailed down the river and out of its mouth near the city of Panama into the Pacific. John Oxenham was thus the first English captain to sail the Pacific, though this achievement is largely forgotten today.

Oxenham sailed south to the Pearl Islands and remained out of sight, waiting for the heavily laden ships passing from the mines in Peru to the city of Panama. After ten days a small vessel hove into view, which Oxenham was able to plunder of some much needed supplies and gold coins to the weight of 60 lbs. Six days later he captured a larger ship carrying 100,000 pesos value in silver bars. With such a magnificent haul acquired so easily Oxenham decided to return to the river, and thence to his ship. It would have been a pity though to leave the vicinity of the Pearl Islands without at least some attempt to take some of the pearls for which the archipelago was renowned.

The natives of the Pearl Island were perhaps no friends of their Spanish overlords but Oxenham's raid quite definitely turned them against him. The natives of the islands immediately sent canoes to the Spanish at Panama to appraise them of the English pirates in their waters, and as Oxenham fled for the river mouth the Spaniards were already setting forth to capture him at the Pearl Islands. When the Spanish, under Captain Juan de Ortega, discovered that Oxenham had already left the islands they sent search parties off in pursuit of him. Word reached Ortega that the English pirates had made their escape up river, but as soon as he began his search Ortega was faced with three rivers falling into one and no clue as to which he should explore. One of the Spaniards spotted a great number of hens' feathers floating down one of the three rivers ahead of them and, assuming them to have been pulled from the hens by the English, Ortega ordered his men up that one. Four days later Ortega's men came upon the English pinnace, pulled up on the sands and guarded by six men. One of the Englishmen was killed and the others fled into the jungle.

Oxenham meanwhile had reached a crisis with his men. He promised his crew their fair share of the treasure once they had returned to England, but first they had to ferry the gold and silver from the pinnace to where they had left the ship. All of the treasure was removed from the pinnace and hidden under branches and brush a mile or more away, then the men set out on the arduous journey, carrying part of the haul through the jungle to their ship. It was clear that several trips would be needed and the men began to grumble, and demanded that the treasure be shared out immediately. Oxenham became angry that his men did not trust him, and declared his intention to find Cimaroons to transport the treasure.

Having found some willing Cimaroons, to the number of around 200, Oxenham was met by the five men who had escaped from the Spanish at the pinnace, and a number of those who had been left to guard the treasure. They reported that the Spanish had not only taken the pinnace but had also found their store of treasure and even now were removing it. This news was all that was needed to unite Oxenham's crew once more, and on the promise of greater shares they set out to recover their loot. Despite outnumbering the Spanish three to one, the English could not defeat the Spanish, who had the advantage of ground, and they were forced to flee empty handed having lost eleven Englishmen and five Cimaroons killed and seven Englishmen captured.

The Spanish returned at once to Panama and sent word to the authorities in Nombre de Dios that Oxenham and his remaining men were making for that part of the coast. Before Oxenham had reached his ship the Spanish had found her and taken her to Nombre de Dios. Oxenham then led his men into the mountains of the Isthmus, where they began to build canoes in the hope of being able to capture a Spanish vessel and so reach home once more. The Spanish however sent 150 men into the mountains to track down and destroy the pirate band. When they came upon the English some were captured and the rest fled with the Cimaroons. The Cimaroons later betrayed the men who had fled with them, and so Oxenham's entire force was captured. Oxenham was asked if he had a letter of marque, and replied that he had not. The crew were all hanged as pirates while Oxenham, two officers and a handful of boys were taken to Lima for interrogation. The officers were unable or unwilling to provide the Spanish with much information about other English attempts on the New World and so were executed. The boys were not executed, but remained prisoners and disappeared into obscurity.

While Oxenham was struggling with his plunder and his crew in the Isthmus of Panama, Drake was at home in Plymouth fitting out five ships for what would become the most famous exploit of the Tudor age[4]. On the 15 November 1577 the *Pelican* of 100 tons led a small squadron consisting of the *Elizabeth* (80 tons), *Marigold* (30 tons), *Swan* (50 tons), and *Christopher* (15 tons), out of Plymouth harbour and down the English Channel. Word had been spread that Drake was to undertake a trading voyage to Alexandria, and one wonders how many of the 164 volunteers aboard the five ships knew that their destination was in fact the Pacific Ocean. Almost immediately a storm drove the ships into Falmouth harbour, and they were forced to sail back to Plymouth to make repairs, not the least of which was the replacement of the flagship's main mast which had had to be cut away. Finally, on 13 December the small fleet was ready to set sail in earnest.

By the time the fleet reached the Atlantic coast of South America they had already lost one boy overboard and one seaman taken captive by Moroccan Arabs. They had captured three ships, one of which replaced the *Christopher*, and one of Drake's personal friends, Thomas Doughty, was under suspicion of trying to incite mutiny. One of the ships had had aboard a very skilled Portuguese navigator named Nuño da Silva who was persuaded to join the enterprise. Shortly after arriving off the South American coast da Silva proved his worth by saving the *Pelican* from wreck during a particularly bad storm.

Six months after leaving Plymouth the fleet reached Port Julian, near the entrance to the Strait of Magellan. The *Swan* and the *Christopher II* had already been stripped of their guns and supplies then abandoned, their crews depleted and their timbers unsound. At Port Julian it was decided to do the same to the *Mary*. It did not escape anyone's notice that it was at Port Julian that Magellan had hanged some of his mutinous crew on his circumnavigation sixty years earlier.

Doughty was becoming more and more of a liability, and by the time the ships were at Port Julian Drake considered that Doughty's presence was endangering the expedition. The entire crews of the remaining vessels were called ashore to witness the trial of Drake's friend for mutiny. There was little doubt that Doughty had tried to stir up disaffection against Drake, but for what reason is not clear. The two men were friends, had known each other for some years, and Drake had given command of one of the prizes to Doughty. Nevertheless, the men chosen by Drake reached the inescapable conclusion that Doughty had tried to stir up mutiny and he was sentenced to death. Before his execution Doughty dined with the other officers and took Holy Communion with Drake.

Although Doughty was not the only man guilty of sedition his execution forcefully reminded all of Drake's authority. Other men associated with Doughty knelt and begged for pardon, and in turn were assured by Drake that there would be no more execution. Two months after arriving at Port Julian the fleet put to sea once more, in better spirits and more united in their enterprise, but reduced to three ships. As they entered the Strait of Magellan Drake changed the name of his ship, in honour of the chief sponsor of the voyage, to the *Golden Hind*.

In early September 1578 the three ships entered the Pacific Ocean, and were at once buffeted by a terrible storm which lasted a month. During this storm the *Marigold* was lost, and Drake was blown south towards Cape Horn. As the *Golden Hind* and *Elizabeth* turned north once more another storm blew up and they too were separated. Captain Winter of the *Elizabeth* steered his ship to safety in the mouth of the Strait of Magellan and remained there for some time, burning huge fires as beacons in the hope that Drake would see them. Contrary winds prevented the *Elizabeth* from entering the Pacific again so after a month or so they reluctantly set out back through the Strait and to England.

After making necessary repairs and despairing of meeting with the *Elizabeth* Drake set off north, towards the coast of Chile and Peru. After plundering a number of ships and sacking the towns of Valparaiso and Arica Drake arrived in the major Peruvian port of Callao, which served the city of Lima. Thirty ships lay in the harbour and Drake was able to sail in amongst them under cover of darkness. At dawn the Spanish realised the identity of the new-comer, but were totally unprepared and so Drake was able to capture two richly laden ships. Here Drake had hoped to be able to rescue his friend John Oxenham from the Inquisition at Lima, but the loss of his companion vessels had left him with insufficient men to force the issue. He had also hoped that his display of force in the harbour, coupled with a letter to the Inquisitors threatening dire reprisals should Oxenham be executed might persuade them to release him, but it was in vain. Realising he could not do more to help Oxenham and hearing of the presence of a fabulous treasure ship en route from Lima to Panama, Drake set out once more.

After a fortnight the treasure ship, nicknamed the *Cacafuego* (Shitfire) was sighted. Drake now employed his cunning. By dragging all the empty barrels he could muster and cramming on all sail Drake gave the *Golden Hind* the appearance of a great lumbering merchantman. When the *Cacafuego* was nearby Drake ordered

the cables which held the drag to be cut and the *Golden Hind*
shot forward and lay alongside the Spaniard. After a brief conversation, during which the Spanish captain could hardly believe his
ears Drake fired a broadside which shot away the Spanish mainmast, then the English pirates boarded and captured her. It took
six days to transfer the treasure from the *Cacafuego* to the *Golden
Hind*, which when catalogued included thirteen chests of plate,
80 lbs of gold, 26 tons of silver and an unspecified amount of precious stones.

After capturing and plundering several more ships Drake knew
that his way back through the Straits of Magellan would be closed
by the Spanish, who were now well alerted to his presence. It may
have been part of Drake's original plan that he should search for
the western end of the fabled North-West passage[5], but now it
certainly seemed to be his most practical course. The *Golden Hind*
sailed as far north as 48 degrees latitude, but finding the coast
continually heading in the wrong direction they concluded that
the Strait of Anian, as the proposed western opening was known,
did not exist. They turned south and anchored for a month in the
vicinity of present day San Francisco.

With the way to the north blocked by the land, and the way to
the south blocked by the Spanish, Drake had no choice but to sail
west. In July 1579 Drake and his crew set out across the Pacific
Ocean. After two months out of sight of land the *Golden Hind*
approached a small group of islands that Magellan had named
'Ladrones'. Despite their desperate need Drake's men could not
land because the natives of the islands were so unfriendly they
even rowed out to attack the ship with stones. On they sailed,
past the Philippines (where Magellan had been killed), and on to
the Portuguese held Moluccas, or Spice Islands. The Portuguese
were involved in a small-scale war with the sultan of the nearby
island of Ternate. Drake sailed for Ternate and befriended the
sultan, by declaring his enmity towards the Portuguese Drake

managed to acquire a monopoly on Ternatean spice for English merchants.

After stopping at a nearby island which he named 'Crab Island' for four weeks to make repairs and prepare the ship for the crossing of the Indian Ocean, the *Golden Hind* set off through the Indonesian islands and out into the open sea. In mid-June 1580 Drake and his band passed the Cape of Good Hope. At the end of July they replenished their stores at Sierra Leone and in September reached Plymouth.

Drake could not have been sure of his reception in England. Amongst his fellow Devonians he was a hero, a giant figure, but he could not know whether the treasure he brought back would be enough to compensate the Queen for the embarrassment his plundering must have caused. Spain was nominally friendly with England, there was no doubt that Drake's actions were those of a pirate, and the Spanish officials in London were quick to point these facts out. In fact, the treasure Drake brought back was more than enough to satisfy the Queen, who had been one of the principal investors. Sir Christopher Hatton, in whose honour the *Pelican* had been renamed *Golden Hind* was equally delighted and was influential at court. Drake's voyage was a success that earned him a fortune and a knighthood.

The way in which Elizabeth overlooked or ignored the protests made by Spain against Drake marked a down turn in the friendship between the two countries, a friendship which had been tolerated for its necessity but which had never been even lukewarm. Other men clamoured to be allowed to follow Drake's example and in 1585 war officially broke out between England and Spain. Henceforth adventurers like Drake did not need to run the risk of being branded pirates. There were fortunes to be made plundering Spanish interests, and now it was legitimate.

4

THE BARBARY PIRATES

Throughout the latter half of Elizabeth's reign the war against Spain provided an outlet for as many young adventurers and soldiers of fortune as wished to try their luck at sea. By the time war broke out officially in 1585 most of the rogues of the West Country had either been captured or had turned their attentions against the enemy. During the war itself hundreds of ships were fitted out and manned on dozens of expeditions. In 1588 for example, only thirty-four of the 226 English ships that fought the Spanish Armada were of the Royal Navy. Even as late as 1596 the thirty-two ships that made up the English contingent of an Anglo-Dutch assault on Cadiz included fourteen privateers, and throughout the conflict privateers were encouraged with vigour. However, in 1603 Elizabeth died and was succeeded by King James VI of Scotland.

James had ruled an impoverished Scotland for twenty years, and now found that instead of becoming King of a wealthy Britain he had merely inherited an England whose exchequer had been ravaged by nearly two decades of war. James himself loathed war and so one of his first decisions as King of England was to seek peace with Spain. In 1604 he achieved this, but the problem remained of what to do with the privateers who had been such an asset and were now a liability. Old letters of marque granting the right to attack the interests of Spain were no longer valid, for Spain was no longer the enemy, and James refused to allow them to be issued again in such large numbers. In any situation where a large group of people suddenly find themselves unemployed at the same time it is to be expected that the crime rate will rise, and that is exactly what happened in the opening years of the seventeenth century.

Apart from the South American trade, including the Spanish treasure flotas, the area that contained the wealthiest shipping, and the most valuable cargoes, was the Mediterranean Sea. Luxuries from the East were carried overland and shipped from the Levant to the rest of Europe. Silks, spices and perfumes were carried in the holds of merchantmen across the clear blue Mediterranean. It is hardly surprising that as James ended the privateering careers of some of the toughest and ablest sea dogs that England has produced, they set their sights on the Mediterranean and the Barbary Coast of North Africa.

The Barbary pirates had been a menace to shipping for centuries, but the sixteenth century was their greatest age. Men like Uruj and Kheir-ed-din Barbarossa, Ochiali, and Dragut had terrorised Christian shipping in the Mediterranean and filled their galleys and the dungeons of Tripoli, Algiers, Tunis and Alexandria with white slaves. The Barbary corsairs had never really succeeded in one respect though, they had never managed to make their presence really felt outside the Strait of Gibraltar. One or two small expeditions had broached the Atlantic, but their ships were not designed for the treatment they were exposed to in the northern waters. It was not until 1585 that the first Barbary corsair sailed out of sight of land in the Atlantic, and in any case it was not practical to take galleys, which required tons of food for the many slaves at the oars, on long voyages.

In the early seventeenth century however the Barbary pirates were joined by a number of renegades from northern Europe, particularly from England and the Netherlands. These renegades took with them knowledge about the techniques of shipbuilding employed in their own countries, and over the next few years the sailing fleets of the North African states grew in size. It is said that a Dutchman named Simon Danseker taught the art of building ocean going vessels to the pirates of Algiers, and that an unnamed Englishman did the same in Tunis. It is quite possible that the Englishman of Tunis was the notorious pirate John Ward, who had earned his living as a fisherman in his native Kent before travelling to Plymouth to join Elizabeth's Navy. At James' accession Ward and a band of his followers stole a ship from Portsmouth harbour and sailed to the Mediterranean where they joined the corsairs and sometimes sailed in consort with Simon Danseker. Alternatively, it may have been one of Ward's other sometime consorts who taught the Tunisians to build European vessels, Plymouth man William Bishop.

Not a great deal is known about Bishop's early life and career, but it can be reasonably assumed that he was one of those many men who had made their livings aboard privateer vessels in Elizabeth's reign. In around 1607 Bishop was in the Mediterranean but was forced to abandon his ship because it was rotten. At Alarica he joined forces with Ward, and met and befriended another associate of Ward's, Anthony Johnson. Bishop and Johnson left Ward's company after a time and began to act together. The Barbary pirates who gave them a safe anchorage and supplies, and possibly their ship as well, required that either Bishop or Johnson always remain behind as a hostage against the other's return. In April 1608 Bishop had acquired enough plunder to fit out his own ship. His crew of around forty were mostly Europeans, men from Flanders, who had joined the Barbary pirates, had been captured by the Venetians and had managed to make their way back once more to Tunis.

At around this time a ship of the Royal Navy and her consort pinnace arrived at Tunis under the command of Captain Henry Pepwell. Pepwell reported that in Tunis harbour at his arrival were Ward, Bishop, and Johnson, together with a John Kerson, William Graves, Samson Denball, Toby Glanfield, a Captain Harris, and Simon Danseker, all renegade pirates. So attractive was the life of these renegades that Pepwell's men began to desert to the pirates, and in the end his losses were so severe that he had no choice but to sell his pinnace, for he had not enough men left to man her. Realising that he could not hope to take any of the pirates by force Pepwell decided to try treachery and guile. There was no question that John Ward was the ringleader of the pirate gangs, and for Pepwell it was clear that if Ward could be captured or killed then the strength of the band would be greatly diminished. He could not do it himself, but if another of the pirates could be persuaded to do it then the strength of the band would be diminished still further.

Pepwell first approached John Kerson, captain of a powerful ship of 300 tons and a man with a sworn hatred for Ward. In exchange for a pardon, which would allow him to return to England and keep his plunder, Kerson agreed to either capture or destroy Ward and his ship. No sooner had these plans been agreed upon than Kerson was sent by the Tunisian authorities to rescue some Tunisian soldiers who had been shipwrecked, and to return them to Tunis. On this voyage however, Kerson had the misfortune to fall in with a powerful Venetian squadron and was killed.

Pepwell required another of the pirates to turn on Ward, and his mind fell on Bishop. From a letter Pepwell wrote after the event we get an interesting glimpse of Bishop's character at that time. Pepwell wrote that he chose Bishop because he:

> was of a different inclination and a better understanding, and had more desire to enjoy his country than the rest; hearing him withal many times complaining of the wrongs Ward had done him, especially detesting his associating with Turks at sea, his taking of Christians and selling them, with divers other outrages.

To Bishop Pepwell offered the same terms as he had to Kerson, that if he could be instrumental in Ward's downfall he could return to England with his plunder. Bishop apparently agreed readily, but as the two men considered their possible courses of action they concluded that Bishop had neither a strong enough ship nor enough men to undertake anything useful against Ward. Pepwell never managed to put an end to Ward, and Bishop remained a pirate.

In the early seventeenth century the English governors in Ireland were in a panic about the number of pirate ships beginning to use the harbours of that realm. Sir Henry Mainwaring, another of the English pirates who used both the Barbary Coast and Ireland as bases claimed that Ireland was the place most frequented by pirates, and explained the attraction. 'Besides that they have all commodities and conveniences that all other places do afford them', he wrote, 'they have also a good store of English, Scottish and Irish wenches which resort unto them, and these are strong attractors to draw the common sort of them thither'. The authorities could do little to prevent the pirates landing where they chose, except to warn the local inhabitants of the dire consequences of consorting with the pirates. The local inhabitants naturally ignored the warnings, for it was known that the pirates would pay two or three times the value for supplies. No direct exchange was ever made, but the pirates would be informed where, say, a bullock or two might be found unguarded at a particular time, and the farmer would be informed where he might find some barrels of wine or suchlike.

In August 1609 a fleet of eleven pirate ships was seen off the western coast of Ireland, with combined crews of 1.000 pirates. The pirates of this fleet elected Bishop as their admiral, and from letters of the time we get another interesting glimpse at the type of man he was. 'A man...' wrote Sir Richard Moryson, 'of such parts and experience in that profession [piracy] that, if his courses of life were any way suitable to them, good use might be made of him in His Majesty's service'. Moryson went on to suggest that Bishop might be a man who could be persuaded to disperse the pirate band before it grew to be uncontrollable. Evidently some approach was made to Bishop, for the next we hear of him is that he has abandoned plans to sack the Newfoundland fishing fleet, and by 1610 was pardoned and was acting as a kind of go-between, helping to negotiate the surrender and pardon of other pirates.

Once the Barbary pirates had acquired the techniques of European shipbuilding a period of terror commenced, in which Barbary pirates might land at any time on almost any coast in their search for slaves. A Dutch renegade named Murat Reis ('Reis' was an approximately equivalent title to 'commodore' amongst the Muslim corsairs) carried out a legendary raid on Baltimore in Ireland, and even as far north as Iceland. White women were particularly prized and the fair Icelandic beauties might have been worth the equivalent of a thousand pounds or more to a corsair like Murat Reis[6]. It is hardly surprising that the West Country suffered heavily from the depredations of these pirates, at sea where fishing and trading vessels were captured, on the coast where commerce was abruptly ended by their presence, and even on the land itself where they carried out their slave raids.

It is amazing to consider how rapidly the Barbary pirates took to raiding outside the Mediterranean. As we've already seen is was not until 1585 that a corsair left sight of land in the Atlantic, and it was not until around 1605 at the earliest that they began to learn how to build and handle ocean going ships. By 1611 though men who had been captured by Barbary pirates off the Scilly Isles were reporting that the corsair fleet in those western waters was forty strong, and had crews to the number of 2,000 pirates. Within a few years the boldness of the pirates had increased to such an extent that they were beginning to make tentative raids into coastal villages.

The middle years of the 1620s seem to have been particularly bad for the people of the West Country. In 1625 a squadron of three Barbary ships captured Lundy Island. The inhabitants of the island were all shipped aboard the pirate vessels to be sold in the slave markets of North Africa. From Lundy the pirates raided the northern coast of Devon and Cornwall, taking slaves from Padstow and other towns before returning to the island base. The merchants and authorities of Bristol were badly shaken, the pirates had threatened to burn Ilfracombe, ships could not be sent on the lucrative Irish trade, and the Newfoundland fishing fleet was expected back at any time.

Fortunately the pirates do not seem to have remained on Lundy for more than a few weeks. Although the island was fairly impregnable in itself a small force such as that of the pirates would have had little chance of holding out for any length of time against a sustained and concerted effort on the part of the Western merchants or the Royal Navy. At the same time however, Barbary pirates were also in the Channel. Sixty captives were snatched from a church in Mount's Bay, and the mayor of Plymouth complained that ships were being taken in the roads. He also believed that 1,000 people had been taken as slaves from Plymouth and the surrounding area in that year alone. That is probably an exaggeration, but even more conservative estimates by later scholars suggest that 1625 was one of the worst years for the depredations of the corsairs and that around 1,000 captives were taken from the West Country as a whole.

The following year the Naval officials based at Plymouth wrote to the government requesting more money. They were inundated, so they wrote, with complaints about the Barbary pirates all along the southern coast, stealing and plundering ships and seizing captives 'whilst the King's ships lie still in harbour, to the charge of the King and the shame of the nation.' One cannot but wonder if this last sentiment was that of the people of the West Country, or of the officials themselves. They went on that the 'pitiful lamentation made by wives and children for their husbands, fathers, and brothers is grievous.' Although the pirates seized captives of all ages and both sexes for the slave markets when they raided ashore it was naturally the men in the ships and boats who bore the brunt of the losses. In ten days in 1626 the Cornish town of Looe lost eighty people, many of them fishermen. So great was the menace that many fishermen simply refused to go to sea.

It must have been cold comfort for the people of Devon when weather forced a Barbary pirate ship commanded by one Jafara Reis into Plymouth harbour. She was instantly seized by the authorities and her crew were thrown into prison. There was no doubt at all that she was a pirate vessel, one of the notorious Sallee rovers who operated from the Moroccan town that now bears the name Rabat, though the crew insisted that they were not Sallee men, but of Algiers. At that time England had an agreement of peace with Algiers, and the King's advocate recommended the release of the men and the return of their ship. Far removed from the day to day reality of the pirate menace the King's advisors in Whitehall agreed with the advocate and ordered the release of the pirates.

Of all the Barbary pirates who ravaged the coasts and shipping of the West Country there is one deserving of specific mention. In the autumn of 1637 seven Sallee rovers were tried in an Admiralty Court of Devonshire, presided over by Sir Edward Seymour and Sir James Bagg. The pirates were known to have captured a vessel in Torbay the previous year, before being driven by bad weather to harbour on the Isle of Wight. These pirates were not so fortunate as their compatriots, and making no attempt to disguise their origin were not released, but instead spent twelve months imprisoned before being tried and found guilty of piracy by the Devon court. Six of the seven men were Muslims, natives of North Africa, but the seventh was a renegade, a Dartmouth man named Thomas Norton.

Norton had been captured by Barbary pirates in around 1620, and was sold in the slave market of Algiers. After some time he managed to escape and made his way overland to the pirate haven of Sallee. At Sallee he found employment in his old trade as a ship's carpenter, and was able sometimes to join piratical expeditions as they set forth. By these means Norton was able to save a considerable amount of money, and when his former owner arrived in Sallee to reclaim him Norton was able to ransom himself. Now a free man, Norton continued to sail with the Barbary pirates, and became a captain of one of the ships. He relished his new life and was 'accounted at Sallee to exceed the Turk's cruelty to his own countrymen'. This latter seems to have been true for in 1636 Norton took a ship of his native Dartmouth. The seamen were taken aboard the pirate ship, destined for the slave market, and the pirates took everything else of use, such as sails, ropes and ammunition. They then cast the Dartmouth ship adrift, and under the gaze of her owners and former crew she was dashed to pieces on the rocks.

Shortly afterwards Norton's own ship was wrecked in a storm off the French coast, and the survivors came ashore at La Rochelle. The French naturally freed the Christian prisoners, but having no quarrel with the pirates allowed them to return to Sallee. Norton himself may have been tired of his life of piracy, or perhaps it was for some other reason that he took a ship for Dartmouth. There he put about that he had managed to escape from Barbary pirates, and he once again took up the trade of a ship-carpenter. Unfortunately for Norton, some of his victims, to whom he had been particularly cruel at Sallee, had also managed to return to Dartmouth and recognised him. He was denounced, arrested and joined the other pirates for trial.

5

A NEW AGE

Not all of the pirates of the early seventeenth century went to the Barbary Coast to pursue their trade. The many small inlets and harbours that had provided such a fine selection of bases to medieval and Tudor pirates of the West Country were just as suited to their descendants in James' reign. Just across the Bristol Channel there were still those ready to deal with the pirates, supplying them with victuals and ammunition for prices way over the odds, and in Ireland too there was little doubt that pirates would receive a warm welcome in most coastal towns and villages. The waters around the West Country were just as dangerous for the honest merchant then as they had been in previous centuries.

Thomas Salkeld, whose name was well known throughout the West in his own time, had been a privateer in Elizabeth's reign, and we know that he had commanded a ship in an expedition against

Spain under the command of Admiral Leveson and Sir William Monson. Unfortunately little other information about his early life has come to light, a pity because he was certainly a most interesting character.

In 1609 Salkeld's names appears among a list of pirates with whom the Lord Admiral himself had been accused of connivance. It appears from this list that Salkeld was an associate of men like Bishop and Jennings, so it is quite probable that he was aboard one of the eleven ships under Bishop's command, or perhaps one of the ten other ships expected that year to join Bishop's gang. When Bishop left the band to receive his pardon some of those captains who elected not to be pardoned went their own way, and Salkeld headed for the Bristol Channel. In early 1610 Salkeld and his crew of sixteen had made themselves infamous locally, and in March of that year crowned their achievements by capturing Lundy.

Perhaps one of the reasons for Salkeld not receiving a pardon at the same time as Bishop and some of his other associates was his personal animosity towards King James. Men like Salkeld felt that they had risked their lives and fortunes in the pursuit of victory over the Spanish. Scotland had been a traditional enemy, even if not an actual enemy. In the early seventeenth century James was a Scottish king making peace with the Spanish, and Salkeld was not alone in his condemnation of James' actions and ideals. Very few however went as far as Salkeld in expressing their opinion, for having taken Lundy, Salkeld declared himself King of an independent nation.

Wishing that he had James' heart on the point of his sword King Thomas of Lundy erected a gallows on the island, from which were hanged all who did not acknowledge his sovereignty. The captives he had taken from ships had their heads shaved and were set to work as slaves, building defences. The government of England took Salkeld's treason seriously enough to send his former commander, Sir William Monson, to Bristol to fit out the thirty-four gun

HMS *Assurance* and retake Lundy. It was expected that Salkeld would realise the hopelessness of trying to hold onto the island with only sixteen supporters and a large party of slaves, who would probably have taken the first opportunity they had to slit Salkeld's throat. However, on arrival at Bristol Monson was informed that Salkeld remained on Lundy, but that the *Assurance* was far from ready for sea. Not wishing to miss the opportunity Monson hired a small vessel, filled it with twenty-five of his men, and set sail immediately.

In the meantime, Salkeld's slaves were growing resentful, and in early April a Bridgwater man named George Escott[7] led a revolt against their captors. It was widely reported that Salkeld had been killed in the revolt, and indeed reports reached Parliament to that effect, but when Monson arrived at Ilfracombe he was informed that Salkeld and his remaining followers had escaped. George Escott was rewarded with a pension for his actions, while Monson set about trying once more to catch Salkeld. Knowing that Salkeld had fled in a hurry, and doubting that his ship was well supplied, Monson expected Salkeld and his men to disguise themselves and put ashore as soon as they could. Word was sent to the mayors, constables and other officials of all the towns and villages on both sides of the Bristol Channel. All strangers were to be quizzed as to where they lived, what business they were in and what they had been doing for the previous month. Monson himself set out to scour the sea. News of Salkeld's fate was not received until some time later, when it was reported that he had met with another notorious pirate, Peter Easton, and joined his crew. The two had quarrelled and Easton had thrown Salkeld overboard.

Peter Easton was a Somerset man who was contracted in 1602 to command a squadron of three ships sent to Newfoundland to protect and keep in order the English fishing fleet there. Like so many privateers Easton turned to piracy when James I made peace with Spain. Over the next few years there are only occasional glimpses of Easton. In 1607 for example we find Easton acting in consort with a Plymouth pirate named Richard Robinson. The following year he and Captain Jennings were involved in an inconclusive action against the twenty-one gun HMS *Tramontana*. In 1609, when Bishop was elected admiral of the eleven-strong pirate fleet in the Irish Sea it seems that Easton was elected his vice admiral. The following year, when Bishop retired from his life of piracy and many of the pirates went their own ways, Easton took over as admiral of those that were left.

In the autumn of 1610 Easton too made overtures to the English authorities in Ireland to obtain a pardon for him and his associates. Copies of his letters were circulated to justices and ministers, and Easton and his men were given a temporary amnesty of forty days while a decision was reached. The pirates were banned from coming ashore in groups of more than two or three at a time, and then only to arrange provisions. On one occasion a larger band of pirates came ashore, so a force of soldiers was sent to arrest them. The pirates fled back to their ships, but the soldiers did succeed in capturing one of Easton's consorts, Captain Gabriel.

While waiting for news of the pardon a squadron of Dutch ships tried to seize Bishop and his ship, lately pardoned, presumably on account of some piracy he had earlier committed against them. When the Dutch ships then entered Falmouth harbour, Easton and his men used this affront as an excuse to cruise in the Channel. Easton claimed that his squadron of nine ships, which was larger than any Royal Navy squadron then at sea, was not powerful enough to face the Dutch, so when he came across two good sized merchantmen he took the opportunity to add them to his fleet. The details of the affair are difficult to untangle. Most naturally accused Easton of committing more piracy against the merchantmen, but Easton claimed that he had only wished to add them to his squadron long enough to fight the Dutch. Whether that was true or not Easton then went on to claim that some seamen from one of the ships then tried to murder him and one of his colleagues as they slept. Forced to defend themselves Easton and some of his pirates killed three or four of the seamen and forced the rest into the other merchant ship. Easton then allowed the other ship to depart with the merchant crews while he himself took command of the larger merchantman. She was a London ship called the *Concord*, and he fitted her with extra guns, presumably taken from the other merchant vessel.

Easton then returned to Ireland to await further news of his pardon. With his fleet now numbering thirteen ships, and having just been reminded by the *Concord* incident of Easton's strength, the authorities in Ireland clamoured for his pardon, so that he would leave their coast in peace. The Naval commander of the area, Captain Skipwith, sent Bishop first to deal with Easton, hoping that the two old friends would arrange some peace and that Easton would be in a more receptive mood at his own arrival. Bishop was fairly successful, some of the pirates agreed to surrender, and when Skipwith arrived himself to talk with Easton he found the pirate ready to hand over the *Concord* and her cargo if he was assured of a pardon.

A general pardon was granted to Easton and the other pirates, but confirmed news of it did not reach them until the deadline set for their surrender had already passed. A squadron was fitted out by the Royal Navy and at the same time as news reached the pirates of this new development they also heard that a Dutch squadron had been sent against them. The pirates hastily distributed as much of their wealth as they could amongst trusted friends and family, some of it was buried, and they sailed away. The nine pirate captains now divided up into three factions. Captains Hewes and Harvey sailed with Easton for Newfoundland[8]. When Easton finally did hear that his pardon had been granted he replied that 'he would not bow to the orders of one King when he himself was, in a way, a King as well[9]

Easton and his consorts made their presence felt on the Newfoundland coast and by the early summer of 1612 had built up their squadron to the number of six ships. At Havre de Grace the pirates stopped to repair their ships, and forced the carpenters out of all the fishing ships in the harbour to aid in the work. Men were recruited and three ships were sent off to stock up with supplies. Some of the pirates left Easton and set off on their own account, but Easton almost certainly made up this shortfall with recruits from the fishing fleet and the settlements. While at Havre de Grace Easton and his men captured Sir Roger Whitbourne, an official with Royal authority, and kept him a prisoner for eleven weeks. During that time Whitbourne endeavoured to persuade Easton to renounce his life of piracy and seek a pardon once again. He met with some success, and when Easton left Newfoundland he sent Captain Harvey aboard a ship for England to seek a general pardon. Easton himself sailed south, and across to the Azores in the hope of intercepting and capturing the Spanish Plate Fleet.

Learning from past mistakes the government lost no time in issuing Easton's pardon and sending it off almost as soon as Harvey had set foot in Ireland. On this occasion that the pardon did not reach Easton was the fault of the 'too much delaying of time' by the messenger. Easton and his men had already been offered a pardon by the Duke of Savoy, who was keen to have such sea dogs in his service. Having failed to take the Plate Fleet Easton entered the Mediterranean and sailed, with four ships and 900 men, to the free port of Villafranca. In 1615 Easton served in the artillery train of the Duke's army, and had such success that he was granted a pension and several other rewards. He converted to Catholicism, married into the Savoyard nobility, obtained the title of Marquis and lived in luxury until his death in around 1620.

Legends abound about Easton and his crew, some of which may be true, others quite likely are not. It is said for example that he rescued a beautiful Irish princess who married his lieutenant,

1   Dartmouth Castle, begun by Sir John Hawley in the late fourteenth century.

2 Lulworth Cove, haunt of the Rogers brothers.

3 One of the alehouses of Studland.

4 Corfe Castle, where John Piers and other pirates were tried in the sixteenth century.

5 Pendennis Castle and Carrick Roads, lair of the Killigrew family.

Drake pevorati novit quem terminus orbis,
Et quem, bis mundi vidit vterq Polus;
Si tacebit homines, facient te Sidera notum,
Sol nescit comites non memor esse sui.

6   Sir John Hawkins, from the
Armada Monument, Plymouth
Hoe.
7   Sir Francis Drake's

monument, Plymouth Hoe.

8   Sir Francis Drake. Frontispiece to *The World Encompassed*, 1635.

9 The *Golden Hind*, a full-scale replica of Drake's famous ship, Brixham, Devon.

12 Buckland Abbey, Drake's home.

10 View along the decks of the *Golden Hind*.

11 One of the *Golden Hind's* guns and tackle.

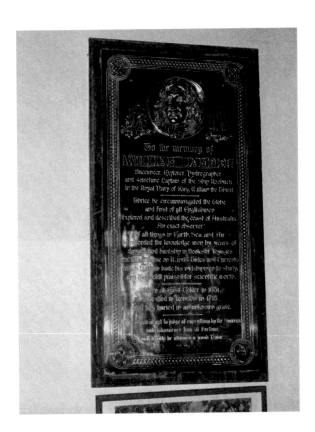

13 Torbay, a superb anchorage used as a base by John Nutt and others.

16 Fashionable Queen's Square in Bristol where Woodes Rogers owned a house.

14 The birthplace of William Dampier, East Coker, Somerset.

18 The Llandoger Trow, supposed meeting place of Daniel Defoe and Alexander Selkirk.

A
VOYAGE
TO THE
South Sea,
AND
Round the World,

Perform'd in the

YEARS 1708, 1709, 1710, and 1711.

Containing

A JOURNAL of all memorable Transactions during the said VOYAGE; the Winds, Currents, and Variation of the Compass; the taking of the Towns of *Puna* and *Guayaquil*, and several PRIZES, one of which a rich *Acapulco* Ship.

A DESCRIPTION of the *American* Coasts, from *Tierra del Fuego* in the *South*, to *California* in the *North*, (from the Coasting-Pilot, a *Spanish* Manuscript.)

An HISTORICAL ACCOUNT of all those Countries from the best AUTHORS.

With a new MAP and DESCRIPTION of the mighty River of the AMAZONS.

Wherein an ACCOUNT is given of Mr. *Alexander Selkirk*, his Manner of living and taming some wild Beasts during the four Years and four Months he liv'd upon the uninhabited Island of *Juan Fernandes*.

Illustrated with CUTS and MAPS.

By Capt. EDWARD COOKE.

LONDON, Printed by *H. M.* for B. LINTOT and R. GOSLING in *Fleet-Street*, A. BETTESWORTH on *London-Bridge*, and W. INNYS in *St. Paul's Church-Yard*. MDCCXII.

Coker.

17 Blue Plaque on the site of
Woodes Rogers' house.

19 The title page of Edward
Cooke's account of Rogers'
circumnavigation, 1712.

20 Henry Avery, woodcut of 1732.

21 Henry Avery, an engraving of 1734.

22 St Andrew's church, Hittisleigh, in which Sam Bellamy was baptised.

23 Craig Long's painting of the
wreck of the *Whydah*.

24 Blackbeard, woodcut of 1732.

25 Blackbeard, engraving of 1734.

Mr. Cheeseman, the couragious Carpenter, that destroy'd Philips the Pyrate and his Crew, is made Carpenter to his Majesty's Ship the Kinsale, as a Reward for his good Services in that brave Enterprize; a particular Account of which may be seen in *The History of the Pyrates*, by Captain JOHNSON.

26 Thomas Anstis, woodcut of 1732.

Gilbert Pike, and bore the first European baby born in Newfoundland. Less fanciful perhaps are the legends that Easton and his pirates built fortifications at Havre de Grace (though the size of the fortifications vary from the quite plausible batteries and basic ramparts to the absurd stone citadel). Or that he fought an action against a French squadron, and that the casualties from this battle lie in a Newfoundland churchyard. Whatever the legends about Easton there is no doubt that the facts of his life are fascinating, and he certainly deserves respect as one of the tiny minority whose piracy actually allowed them to live in riches instead of being hanged in rags.

The early seventeenth century was certainly a time of fascinating pirates, but perhaps the most intriguing was John Nutt of Topsham or Lympstone. Like so many pirates we only have occasional glimpses of his early life, but it appears that in around 1620 he was gunner aboard a Dartmouth ship acting as a kind of seaborne mercenary, or hired thug, in the pay of Sir George Calvert. Calvert, later Lord Baltimore, was in the process of trying to build a colony in Newfoundland, and Nutt was one of those hired to help protect it.

While his ship was in Newfoundland waters Nutt collected together a band of men and seized a French ship. Fitting out the French ship for his piratical needs Nutt quickly captured a larger ship from Plymouth and transferred himself to her. Shortly afterwards he added a Flemish ship of around 200 tons to his force and set about plundering the ships of the Newfoundland fishing grounds[10]. After two years of piracy Nutt returned to English waters, confident that he was strong enough in force to resist any attempts to capture him. In the opening months of 1623 Nutt assured himself of local popularity and support by ferrying large numbers of seamen to Newfoundland to escape the press gangs which Sir John Eliot, Vice Admiral of Devon, had sent out in Plymouth and other Devon ports. Nutt was less popular with the mayors and other worthy dignitaries of the West Country and Wales, and their complaints about his depredations are manifold. From his base in Torbay Nutt was seemingly able to plunder shipping at will.

Nutt, like so many of the pirates of that time, was desperate for a pardon. He hoped that in exchange for giving up his life of piracy and becoming a model citizen, perhaps even serving the crown, he would be allowed not only to escape unpunished, but also to keep some or all of the plunder he had amassed. In fact, two pardons were issued to him, but one way or another he was not in a position to fulfil their terms within the allotted deadline on either occasion. In the middle of 1623 however Nutt was visiting Torbay more and more frequently, to visit his wife and children there and to seek news of a pardon. With the number of complaints from as far afield as Ireland growing, Sir John Eliot was sent orders to capture Nutt by whatever means he could, and as discreetly as he could. Eliot was instructed to familiarise himself with Nutt's friends and the places he visited to drink when he was ashore. Instructions were to be sent to the justices and constables around the coast to keep a careful watch on all seamen coming ashore and to apprehend any of whom they were suspicious, though Nutt was not named personally.

These orders did not reach Eliot until much later, but Eliot had already taken it upon himself to capture Nutt, and set about doing so by intrigue. At the end of May Eliot managed to make Nutt believe that he was in possession of a valid pardon for him and his crew. Nutt wrote to Eliot from Torbay, where he lay anchored in his ship of fourteen guns, that he was prepared to pay a £300 fine in exchange for his pardon, and that he wished to meet with Eliot ashore to discuss it. Eliot immediately rode from Plymouth to Dartmouth to entice Nutt ashore, but evidently the pirate had lost some of his nerve for he claimed that his crew would not let him leave the ship.

On 6 June Eliot therefore agreed to meet with Nutt aboard his ship in Torbay. While Nutt had been seeking his pardon in

Torbay he had seized the *Edward and John* of Colchester, and Eliot insisted that it should be returned to its owners. For a whole day the two men negotiated, Nutt trying to gain a pardon on terms which would suit him, and Eliot trying to convince Nutt to surrender himself for a pardon which did not exist. Eventually it was agreed that Nutt would pay a fine of £500, would hand over six packs of calf skins to Eliot's deputies, and would surrender his ship. No mention was made of the Colchester ship in the final arrangement.

Nutt's suspicions were not entirely assuaged, and even as his ship lay at the mouth of Dartmouth harbour he sent word to Eliot that he had been told his pardon was no longer valid. Eliot wrote back to soothe him, so Nutt sailed into Dartmouth. Nutt was not arrested immediately, Eliot knew he would try to make an escape as long as he thought he had the King's pardon. The mayor of Dartmouth saw to it that the sails and some of the rigging were removed from Nutt's ship to prevent him venturing forth to plunder the shipping, some of which was only now moving because its owners knew that Nutt was no longer at sea. Nutt's men were dressed in the clothes they had stripped from the crew of the *Edward and John*, and they paraded up and down through the streets and taverns of Dartmouth bragging about their plunder and their pardon.

Within a few days Eliot received orders to send Nutt to London to be tried and to imprison his crew. All of the plunder was removed from Nutt's ship, and several chests of goods were recovered from the countryside around, where they had been landed and lodged with friends and associates before Nutt's surrender. Eliot was called to court to explain the matter to the King himself.

Amongst the plunder that Eliot took into his custody was the Colchester ship and her cargo that Nutt had taken only shortly before his surrender. On the occasion of Eliot's visit to Nutt's ship the master of the *Edward and John* had pleaded with Eliot to intervene on his behalf, but Eliot had either refused or not been able.

Now, towards the end of June, orders came from the Admiralty Court to Eliot and to the mayor of Dartmouth to see that the ship was at last returned to her owners. Eliot had hoped to use the *Edward and John* as a lever to make Nutt give up more of his vast wealth and, sure of his friends at court, refused the order. Within the month Eliot had been arrested and was imprisoned at the Marshalsea.

His refusal to obey the order he had been sent was not the cause of the arrest, though it hardly won him any friends. As the investigation into Nutt's piracy had been progressing the master of the *Edward and John* claimed that Nutt had not removed anything from the ship, but that when Eliot had joined him they had looted her together and taken fourteen chests of sugar. This charge was untrue, and the owners of the vessel later testified that she and her cargo had been returned entirely intact. What had prompted the master to make the claim in unclear, but it is possible that he was persuaded into it somehow by Nutt or one of his friends. Eliot denied the claim, and with the testimony of the owners it was dropped.

When Nutt was examined himself he admitted that he had taken some chests of sugar, and that Eliot had not been present. But he went on to say that Eliot had told him if he did not have the money to pay his fine then he should find it 'howsoever he came to it'. Nutt added that Eliot's deputy, Richard Randall of Dartmouth, had brought messages from Eliot informing him of rich Spanish ships lying in Dartmouth Harbour, and suggesting that he might seize them. Randall denied this and other charges of encouraging Nutt to further piracy, but did admit to mentioning in conversation the rich Spanish vessels. Eliot denied all the accusations of connivance and pointed out throughout his examination that everything he had done was carefully designed to bring Nutt peaceably into Dartmouth to surrender.

The case was considered very carefully. Nutt was undoubtedly a rogue and a pirate, but he had made similar accusations about the

Vice-Admiral of Devon. These accusations could not be proven, and though Eliot was certainly innocent he was unable to disprove them. The behaviour of Randall was negligent at best, and possibly pointed towards Eliot's guilt. Based on the testimony of the three men involved no satisfactory conclusions could be drawn, and the people involved began to look for other things on which to base their subsequent actions. The Lord Admiral, the Duke of Buckingham, was at sea, and only he had the power to appoint a new Vice Admiral of Devon. Since the vice admiral held a vital and busy post perhaps it might have been wise to release Eliot, at least until Buckingham's return. Both Eliot and Nutt now learned the true value of their friends at court, and if the connivance with pirates in the Tudor age by officials was incredible it was nothing compared to the support Nutt now found. Sir George Calvert, Nutt's former employer and now a Secretary of State, wrote personally to the King outlining the good reasons to pardon Nutt. A pardon had already been given, and it was through no fault of Nutt's that he had not received it; Nutt would be a very useful man to have in the King's service; Nutt had surrendered voluntarily and had not committed any piracy since hearing of his pardon. All these were reasons that contributed to Nutt's pardon, issued by the King on the 18 August 1623.

Eliot had high hopes of his own release. He believed he had acquitted himself well at his examination, and that the need for his personal presence to oversee the maritime affairs of Devon was well known. Before orders could be given for his release the council broke for a vacation, and Eliot was destined to remain in the Marshalsea until they reconvened. Desperate now, Eliot wrote to Secretary of State Conway, whom he believed to be his friend outlining the reasons that he should be released. Conway's reply informed Eliot that he had made powerful enemies at Court. Calvert was convinced that Eliot was deliberately working against him. Other lords were shocked by Eliot's deviousness in the capture of Nutt, and the underhand way in which he used a Royal grant. It is not clear when exactly Eliot was released but the probability is that it was in October of 1623, he was definitely free by November. It must have been a great insult to him that while he languished in prison awaiting his fate, Nutt was enjoying his freedom, and actually sued Eliot for £100 in compensation for his seized assets.

The next we hear of John Nutt he seems to be proving some truth in Calvert's assessment of him. In January 1627 Nutt is recorded as having taken command of the privateer vessel *Mary Margaret* of his native Topsham. Four months later we are introduced to John Nutt's brother, Robert, as owner and captain of the privateer *Mary*. It was probably in the *Mary* that Robert Nutt committed what appears to be his first act of piracy, the taking of a London pinnace, the *Elizabeth*. Robert carried his prize into Dartmouth Harbour where the judge of the local Admiralty Court, William Kift (who had been instrumental in the seizing of John Nutt's plunder in 1623), immediately declared the goods as piratical.

The case for piracy against Robert Nutt seems to have gone no further than arrangements for restitution of the pinnace to its owners. Only six weeks after first receiving his letter of marque Robert Nutt had given up command of the *Mary* in favour of the slightly larger privateer *Trial*, of Dartmouth. Shortly afterwards John also took command of a larger ship, the *London*. The following year John Nutt was cruising in the Channel with a Captain Stevens when they came upon the *Black Dog* of Rotterdam, and took her. They took her to Southampton and there followed a long legal battle which resulted in the prize being restored to her owners. It is impossible to tell which of the Nutt brothers was responsible for the capture of a Portuguese ship which was taken into Topsham and reputed to have a cargo worth £10,000 aboard. John Nutt's activities as a privateer appear to have earned him a fine sum of money, in 1629 he took command of a still larger vessel, the *Regard* of Topsham, while his brother had the command of the *Diamond* of Dartmouth, both owned by consortia of Devon merchants. The following year John was able to go into the business himself, and two ships actually owned by him were granted letters of marque. He took command of the largest himself, the *Swan*, while the smaller *Goose* acted as his consort.

One other privateer whose name appears as the owner and captain of several ships granted letters of marque at this time is Jonathon Downes. In 1626 Downes was the owner and captain of the *Speedwell* of London, and two years later he owned and commanded the *Marygold* of Weymouth. Towards the end of 1630 a letter of marque was granted to the *Niger* of Weymouth, owned by Downes who was possibly also her captain. If he was also her captain then it was probably in this ship that he began his piratical career in the early months of 1631.

In around May 1631 Downes met up with Robert Nutt and the two sailed in consort in the Channel and the Irish Sea, probably under Downes' command. The following month Downes was captured off the Isle of Man and Robert Nutt made for the Channel once more. Nutt only had a small vessel, but towards the end of June he managed to capture the *St. Anthony* of 300 tons and twenty-six guns. Off the Welsh coast Nutt put the merchant and his crew into his small vessel and took the heavy, well-armed ship for himself. In early July Nutt landed at Pwllheli in Wales and spent some time trading with the inhabitants there, much to the chagrin of the local authorities who had insufficient forces to prevent him.

Some time in early 1632 Robert Nutt fell in with another band of pirates commanded by Captain Norman, and a third commanded by Captain Smyth. Norman also used Pwllheli as a base from which to operate and in which to sell his plunder, and it is possible the two pirates met there. At around this time Nutt took a French ship and used her to house most of the prisoners he had taken from other ships. Some of the prisoners managed to take the ship and deliberately ran her aground on the Irish coast, where they were promptly arrested as pirates. They were transferred to Bristol where, after being examined, they were set free. Nutt and Norman themselves were at Crookhaven in County Cork at this time, offloading some of their plunder, believed to include 'gold, pearl, unicorns' horn… [and] elephants' teeth'.

In March Robert Nutt and his associates were pardoned by the King, and were given a deadline by which they were to surrender themselves. At the same time instructions were sent to two captain, one of the Navy and one a privateer, to apprehend Nutt and Norman if'they shall be so wedded to their lewd courses as to refuse to come in within the time limited'. The two captains charged to deliver Nutt and Norman to justice were Thomas Kettleby of the Royal Navy, and John Nutt. In May Robert wrecked the *St. Anthony* on the Irish coast, possibly deliberately as an excuse not to surrender within the deadline. He shipped himself in a smaller vessel of only three guns and was reported to have sailed for the shoals and islands of the Flemish coast. Kettleby remained at his post at Plymouth while John Nutt went chasing after his brother with his pardon. It was widely rumoured that 'when the one brother finds out the other he will join with him in that very devilish trade.'

John Nutt almost certainly did not find his brother, and it is doubtful whether Robert had in fact gone to Flanders at all. In July of that year Robert Nutt was again causing headaches among the captains of the Royal Navy squadrons sent to apprehend him. He was reported as being off the coast of Spain while Captain Smyth, was temporarily using Lundy as a base where he awaited the ships of Irish trade. Captain Plumleigh with HMS *Assurance* was sent to the West to catch Nutt and Norman, and expected Nutt to be sailing for Crookhaven where he had a wife.

Plumleigh may have been correct for the next month Nutt was reported in St George's Channel between Ireland and Wales. He may have been visiting his family at Crookhaven, but in the middle of the month Nutt was once more at Pwllheli selling off the cargo of a prize he had taken. Plumleigh meanwhile only just missed catching Smyth at Lundy. In late August Nutt and one of his consorts were said to be off the Isle of Bute, in Scotland. Plumleigh immediately set out after them, and despite adverse weather and tides was able to catch up with them. Nutt and his consort spotted Plumleigh, and taking HMS *Assurance* to be a merchantman sailed up to try to board her. Realising their mistake in time the pirates turned and fled. Plumleigh fired thirty shots at the pirates, and was assured that ten had pierced Nutt's ship, and probably a similar amount in Nutt's consort. The pirates did not wait to fire back, but used their faster ships to flee and within three or four hours were out of sight of Plumleigh.

Plumleigh reported the incident with some pride to his superiors and went on hunting for Nutt. In October Plumleigh found Nutt, but this time Nutt was expecting him. Plumleigh had with him HMS *Assurance* of thirty-four guns, and as consorts two of the *Lion's Whelps*, fourteen gun ships which had been built in the style of Dunkirk privateer frigates, and which were noted for their speed and handiness. This squadron would have been a fine force for dealing with Nutt, indeed after their encounter in August Plumleigh maintained that with the firepower of the *Assurance* and speed of one of the *Whelps* Nutt would not have been able to get away. It was possibly because of that report that Plumleigh now had command of the two *Whelps*, but had he been able to foresee his next encounter with Nutt he would have requested a considerably larger force. Nutt had joined forces with some Barbary pirates operating in the Irish Sea and now had a squadron of twenty-eight ships at his disposal[11]. The engagement that followed was short and Plumleigh naturally turned tail and fled. On this occasion Plumleigh had the heels of Nutt and was able to get away without any of his ships being either captured or sunk.

After such an obvious challenge to the authorities Nutt could not safely remain in English waters and fled to Spain. During his career Nutt had plundered freely from ships of any nation, so he could expect little protection from the Spanish. In November 1632 news reached England that Nutt had been captured and hanged at Corunna, and the following month one of Nutt's officers was captured and imprisoned aboard HMS *Victory*. Captain Norman was still at large and in December was reported as being in the Limerick River. In March 1633 Norman was still of the Irish coast plundering ships, but by June he had left English waters in a leaky ship and in July was reported drowned.

That should have been the end of Robert Nutt's story, but in early 1636 a final twist was added. In February that year a Spanish ship was driven by bad weather into Falmouth. Aboard the ship, which was carrying military supplies, were three English officers, two gunners and a navigator. Their names were Stephen Willing, John Billing and Robert Nutt. Willing and Billing had been members of Nutt's crew and somehow the three of them had escaped execution. All three were arrested at Penryn and put into safe keeping, but their eventual fate remains unknown at present. John Nutt is last heard of as lieutenant of a privateer in 1653.

6

THE WORLD TURNED UPSIDE DOWN

In 1642 the differences of opinion which existed between King Charles I and his advisors on one hand the Parliament on the other boiled over, and in August the Civil War which had been threatening finally broke out. The English Civil War affected all parts of the British Isles, not just England but Ireland and Scotland, the Channel Islands, and even the New World colonies. Naturally the West Country had a part to play in the conflict, and in the first years of the war the area was particularly affected. Most of Cornwall, and much of Devon and Dorset were in favour of the King, but even in these areas the centres of commerce which were governed by mercantile and municipal dignitaries usually declared for Parliament. Because of the dominance of Bristol on Somerset trade that county was more inclined to favour Parliament. So it was that at the outbreak of war the West Country consisted of

Parliamentarian strongholds at Plymouth, Exeter, Dartmouth, Poole, Barnstaple, Bridgwater, Bristol, and other places, in the middle of largely Royalist counties.

At the same time, most of the standing fleet of the Royal Navy also declared for Parliament, and the King was left without a cohesive naval force. A small handful of ships and men remained loyal to the King, and several Royalist merchants fitted out their ships in his service, but with few ports under his control anywhere in the country their effectiveness was limited.

One by one, as campaigns on land progressed, the harbour towns of the West Country changed sides. Falmouth had been held for the King since the beginning of the war, and the Cornish Royalists laid siege to Plymouth and Exeter fairly early. In June 1643 Bridgwater surrendered to the Royalists and Bristol was taken after a fierce battle the following month. In August the Royalists took Weymouth and Portland, and Barnstaple and Bideford both fell in September, along with Appledore. That same month Exeter finally succumbed to the Royalists, though their attempt to storm Poole met with disaster. In October the Royalists were able to take Dartmouth, but their detour there probably cost them the chance to take Plymouth. Plymouth in fact remained under siege for four years, but was never taken. In 1644 the Royalists involved themselves in a futile siege of Lyme, and Portland and Weymouth were recaptured for Parliament. Elsewhere in the country the war was turning bad for the King and in the middle of 1645 the fearsome New Model Army reached the West Country. Bridgwater was retaken in July and Bristol fell after a second stiff fight in September. In January 1646 the New Model Army took Dartmouth and in April the Royalist garrisons of Barnstaple, Salcombe and Exeter surrendered. Falmouth remained the only Royalist stronghold in the West Country mainland until it too fell in August, and in September Lundy and the Scilly Isles were forced to capitulate.

During the time that the Royalists held key ports like Dartmouth and Bristol they were used as bases by privateers and pirates, who were offered a kind of dubious legality in return for a dubious service. Some of these privateers were almost formed into a fleet by the King's Admiral, Sir John Pennington, but they never really achieved much more than to operate as squadrons of commerce raiders, plundering ships from Parliamentarian held ports and disrupting the supply of Parliament's army. Whether these men were pirates or privateers is open to debate. On the one hand they were authorised by the King or his deputies, acted like privateers and only attacked (for the most part) the enemies of their sponsor, and a share of their plunder was used to support the Royalist cause. On the other hand the King himself did not actually have the power to grant commissions to privateers, that was the exclusive preserve of the Lord Admiral (or his deputies), and the Lord Admiral had sided with Parliament at the outbreak of war. This might seem like a dubious legal question, but the fact remains that the Royalist privateers were always described as pirates by their Parliamentarian enemies, and at least one was hanged for piracy for his actions in the Civil War[12]. While some of the privateer commanders were gentlemen, there is no doubt that a number were cut-throats who would have probably turned to piracy or some other unsavoury profession had they not found employment in the Royalist ranks.

Almost as soon as they were able the Royalists of the West Country set about fitting out privateers, and even as early as the end of 1642 Sir Nicholas Slanning armed a ship which had been blown into Falmouth Harbour and sent her to sea as the *Michael*. The following year, when Sir Ralph Hopton led the Cornish army into Devon he captured a sixteen-gun ship, the *Frederick and William*, at Saltash, and she too was sent to sea.

One of the most significant of these early privateers was Richard Jones, a Falmouth man who in April 1643 was cruising off the French coast near Brest and taking considerable profits.

Along with Jones was another ship, the *Mayflower*, commanded by Captain Polhill. Jones and Polhill used a simple method to capture their prey. The two ships would wait in near the shore where lookouts were posted. The lookouts passed the word if any ships were sighted flying English colours, whereat Jones and Polhill would put to sea and take their prize.

By June Jones and Polhill had added a third ship to their fleet, a Yarmouth ship which they had armed with ten guns. So successful had they become at their trade that Parliament sent two ships, the *Eighth Whelp*[13] and the *Charity*, to hunt them down. The two ships arrived off the French coast and were quickly given intelligence about the methods employed by Jones and Polhill. Accordingly the captains of the *Whelp* and the *Charity* disguised their ships as merchantmen and sailed to Brest where they were spotted by Jones and Polhill's lookouts. The day after their arrival the two naval ships were approached by a boatload of armed men, who appeared intent on boarding the *Charity*, but in fact attacked neither ship. The following day another boat arrived, this one carrying a man who enquired as to the identity of the two newcomers. The man, it later transpired, was Polhill's lieutenant, and the captains of the naval ships stuck to their story that they were merchantmen on their way to London who had taken refuge in Brest from some Barbary pirates who had chased them. A short time later Polhill's ship set sail with her guns run out and her men armed. She sailed towards the two ships Polhill intended to take as prizes but at the last moment the *Eighth Whelp* set sail, ran out her guns and cut her anchor cable. The captain of the *Whelp* ran up his true colours and set about to chase Polhill, who ran his ship aground. The *Whelp* anchored only a couple of hundred yards from the *Mayflower* and the two ships began to pound one another with their broadsides. After an hour-and-a-half the privateers struck their colours and hoisted a white flag. The *Charity* then laid alongside the *Mayflower* to take possession of her, but found that Polhill and one of his officers had escaped through a gun port some time previously. After the battle around forty men from Jones' and Polhill's crew surrendered themselves to the Captain of the *Eighth Whelp* and were allowed to join her crew. Although Polhill later had command of another Royalist ship it seems that Jones retired.

When the Royalists captured Bristol in July 1643 it should have given them an opportunity to build up a proper cohesive fleet, but they squandered their chance and only two privateers, the *Fellowship* and the *Hart* were sent out to try to secure the Bristol Channel and St George's Channel. Although the *Fellowship* was a fairly large and strong ship they were both taken within a month at Milford Haven, in very similar circumstances to Polhill's. Both ships were run aground and after a short exchange of broadsides the Royalists surrendered and many of the men joined the crews of their captors.

It was the ports on the south coast of the West Country which contributed the most to the Royalist efforts at sea at this time, and after the fall of Dartmouth in October several ships were added to the Royalist lists. One ship, the *George*, commanded by Captain George Bowden, had formerly been a privateer in Parliamentarian service, but Bowden declared for the Royalists and arrived at Dartmouth only a few days after the town's capture. Almost at once Bowden was at sea again. He shortly met with a squadron of Scottish ships, accompanied by one of London. Bowden called on the London ship to surrender to him, but the crews of the Scottish ships threatened in turn to board the *George* if he tried. Being outnumbered Bowden sailed away, but followed the squadron at a discreet distance. The following day, off La Rochelle, one of the Scottish ships became separated from the others. Bowden took his opportunity and rushed down upon her and boarded. She was found to have aboard a good cargo of rye, tallow and butter which Bowden took, along with the prize to the Scilly Isles, and then into Dartmouth.

Also at Dartmouth at around this time the Royalists began to form a squadron under the command of the Earl of Marlborough. In December Marlborough took command of some of the ships that had been captured in the harbour when the town fell, and the King himself asked the people of Dartmouth to assist in the fitting out of Marlborough's squadron. In January 1644 the master of a merchantman that had been captured and taken into Dartmouth managed to report to Parliament that there was a multitude of ships there:

> Preparing ... to go for the Canary Islands and Madeira and the Azores to seize on any English ships there, and thence to the Isle of May and the Cape Verde Islands, and so to seize all English ships found trading there, and to secure all those plantations to themselves against the King and Parliament, and so to pass northwards by Virginia, New England and Newfoundland, there to take all fishermen that are for the Parliament, with which ships and men they intend to make a complete fleet to set on against the Parliament and to master the Narrow Seas.

The Lord Admiral sent word to Parliament about this new menace, afraid that if the Royalists reached the West Indies they might find 260 ships there to join their cause, a force against which he could not possibly compete for naval mastery. Six ships under the command of Captain Jordan were hastily dispatched to catch up with Marlborough and prevent him crossing the Atlantic.

In actual fact Marlborough had set sail with only three ships, and only as far as St Malo in France. The people of Guernsey sent word to Jordan, and he lay in wait for Marlborough's return at the Channel Islands. Marlborough had been bringing back some supply ships from France, and these had been sent on ahead to Dartmouth when the Royalists realised the presence of Jordan's ships. Marlborough's ships shortened sail ready to give battle and the Parliamentarians fired a broadside at them. The range was extreme however and the shot merely plopped into the sea between the ships. Night was coming on so Marlborough made for the safety of St Aubin's Bay in Jersey, protected by the guns of the Royalist held Elizabeth Castle. Jordan dared not enter the bay so waited outside until the next day. Some of Marlborough's men went ashore that evening and could not be found the next morning. Without enough men to man his guns Marlborough remained in St Aubin's bay for another day while Jordan waited off shore. On the third morning at dawn Marlborough set sail, but by that time Jordan had clearly tired of his task. His ships were nowhere to be seen and Marlborough was able to return to Dartmouth without confrontation.

Early in January 1645 the East Indiaman *John* sailed into Bristol and offered to join the Royalists. Only a short time before she had been at the Cape of Good Hope and John Mucknell, the sailing master, found that divisions were strong among the crew as to whether they supported the King or Parliament. Mucknell himself supported the King and decided to take the *John* for Royalist service.

Mucknell invited the captain and the other men who supported Parliament to a feast on an island. When his guests were well fed and well drunk a prearranged message arrived for Mucknell that the men left on the ship were causing trouble, so Mucknell left the party to calm things down on the ship. Mucknell never returned to the island, despite the cries of distress and fires made by the twenty-three men left marooned there. Onboard the ship there still remained a handful of men who supported Parliament, and these men, according to a Parliamentarian report of the events, had their ears nailed to the mainmast before Mucknell cut them off. Once he had control of the ship Mucknell hoisted sail and set course for Bristol

The *John* had been seen cruising off Dover where Mucknell 'took away some persons when he had invited them aboard him

by a weft'[14], before sailing north and cruising off the coast of
East Anglia. Mucknell's arrival in the North Sea was a momen-
tous occasion, his ship, the *John*, was probably the largest ship in
Royalist hands and is described as 'about 500 tons, fore and aft
with long galleries and about 40 pieces of ordnance'. In 1645 the
largest ship in the Parliamentarian Summer Guard was the *James* of
forty-eight guns, followed by Admiral Batten's flagship, the forty-
two gun *St Andrew*. The only other ship in Parliament's fleet that
carried more than forty guns was Swanley's *Lion* in the Irish Sea.
The whole of East Anglia was alerted to Mucknell's presence, the
bailiffs of Yarmouth were instructed to order the captains of all
the Parliamentarian ships in the harbour and roads of Yarmouth
to put to sea to join in the search for Mucknell, and were in turn
instructed to pass the orders along to any other Parliamentarian
ship they met with.

Shortly afterwards a squadron of three ships under the command
of Captain Joseph Jordan caught up with Mucknell in the Channel.
The combined guns of the Parliamentarian ships numbered sev-
enty-six, which combined with the greater manoeuvrability of
three ships over one in a skirmish should have made the defeat
of the *John* a simple matter. About four o'clock the eighteen-gun
Cygnet came up with the *John* and Captain Mann called out offering Mucknell quarter, whereupon Mucknell stabbed his sword
into the deck at his feet and declared he would ask for no quarter.
Broadsides were exchanged and soon the *Constant Warwick* and
Expedition arrived and joined the fight. Jordan was soon wounded
in the leg and the *Expedition* retired from the fight after only firing
two broadsides.

Captain Gilson sailed the *Constant Warwick* right alongside the
John and offered £10 to any man who could pull the flag from
the *John's* mainmast. Ten pounds would have amounted to around
six weeks wages for the captain of a ship such as the Constant
Warwick, and over a year's wages for a common seaman, so it was

well worth the risk for a brave man to take. Two men were brave enough and though one fell overboard and drowned in the attempt the other got aboard the *John* and scrambled up the shrouds toward the flag. At this crucial moment however the rope holding the two ships together gave way, or was cut, and the ships parted leaving the brave seaman stranded aboard the *John*. For two hours the Royalists were unaware that one of the enemy was hiding in their main fighting top, and when they discovered him there they persuaded him to come down. Not satisfied with his day's adventures the seaman then sought more by taking the first opportunity to escape that presented itself and stole the *John's* longboat. Mucknell then brought the John up once more with the *Constant Warwick* and *Cygnet* and continued to fire his cannons at both vessels before the skirmish was broken off after three or four hours of fighting. Mucknell escaped in the night, but his ship was run aground on the Scillies by the carelessness of his pilot. In the Parliamentarian fleet blame began to be apportioned for the failure despite very favourable odds of the three ships to capture Mucknell. Jordan, who had withdrawn the *Expedition* (the most powerful of the three ships) early in the skirmish received most of the blame.

During the Civil War was it was not just English pirates and privateers who used the West Country ports. At about the same time as Parliamentarian ships were being sent hastily after Mucknell and Bowden in the North Sea and the Channel a squadron of Dutch privateers commanded by one Jan van Haesdonck entered Falmouth with eight prizes, thirty prisoners and an enormous quantity of military supplies. It was said that van Haesdonck refused to remain in Falmouth and put to sea again straight away, but he soon returned with prizes worth around £3-4,000. Later that year some effort seems to have been made to gather all of the privateers together at Falmouth under van Haesdonck's command. This force was then to be used to take Guernsey which could be used, with Jersey, as a base for hundreds of privateers to disrupt Parliamentarian trade with the Continent. Nothing came of this plan, but several ships do seem to have joined van Haesdonck, including that commanded by Francis Fourther who had been Bowden's lieutenant.

With the fall of the ports in the West Country the use of the privateers was limited. They had no bases, except overseas, from which to work, and the money and supplies which they generated could not be passed on to the Royalists on land. The Civil War was fast being lost by the Royalists, and although various uprisings occurred and pockets of resistance remained, the latter part of the civil war, between 1645 and 1651 was a succession of acts of desperation on the part of the Royalists. A number of privateers worked successfully from Ireland, and following the fleet mutiny of 1648 a small squadron led by the King's nephew Prince Rupert operated for four years, but none of these forces had the effect of the privateers of 1642-45.

7

THE CIRCUMNAVIGATORS

At around the time that Prince Rupert was recrossing the Atlantic after a fruitless cruise in the Caribbean there was born in the village of East Coker, Somerset, a child named William Dampier. While still a child Dampier's parents both died, and at the age of seventeen he was sent to sea by his guardians on a Weymouth ship to France and then to Newfoundland. Disliking the cold he experienced on this voyage young Dampier made another, to the East Indies, before he joined the Royal Navy in around 1673. Dampier fought aboard the *Royal Prince*, flagship of Sir Edward Spragge, at the two battles of the Schoonveld that year, but falling ill he was placed aboard a hospital ship. From his sick berth he was a witness to the battle of the Texel, in which Spragge was killed.

The following year Dampier was offered employment by one of his neighbours at East Coker, as an under manager of a plantation in Jamaica. Dampier remained in this position for six months before he received a better offer and travelled to the other side of Jamaica to manage a plantation belonging to a Captain Hemming. The position there was clearly not what Dampier was expecting, nor was he suited to it, and as soon as he was able he extricated himself and returned to the sea in a succession of coasting vessels around the island.

In 1675 Dampier was aboard a small vessel engaged in the logwood trade with Campeche. The heart of the logwood tree (*Haematoxylum campechianum*) had been discovered to produce an excellent red dye in the sixteenth century, and among the earliest English semi-permanent settlements in the New World were logging posts in Campeche and the surrounding area, in what is now Belize. It was estimated that one ton of useable wood was worth £100 in Europe, though in Dampier's time the logwood cutters sold it to the merchants for £5 per ton. Almost as soon as Dampier returned from his first voyage to Campeche he signed aboard another ship for the same journey, this time with the intention of remaining there to cut logwood himself.

Amongst the logwood cutters of Campeche (of which Dampier tells us there were between 250 and 260) were a number of men who had been privateers until the end of the war with Spain. Now unemployed they had taken to logwood cutting, but their old habits died hard and they frequently raided local native settlements, and their drinking bouts were the stuff of legend. Many of these men were captured by the Spanish, but Dampier was able to stay on in Campeche a little while longer. After a particularly bad storm, and with no money to buy provisions, Dampier was forced to join a band of privateers. The privateers' voyage was not a success, but it enabled Dampier to return to logwood cutting for a few months before he returned to England in 1678.

Dampier's movements in England are not clear, but they included marriage to Judith, a servant of the Duchess of Arlington. He did not remain long and within six months was aboard a ship returning to the West Indies. He carried with him some goods which he intended to sell in Jamaica, and to use the proceeds to buy more goods which he could sell to the logwood cutters of Campeche. Once in Campeche he would then continue there as a logwood cutter himself. However, once in Jamaica Dampier rethought his plans and used the profits from his sales to buy himself a small estate in Dorset, to which he intended to return at the end of 1679. However, having spent all of his money he was persuaded to go on a trading voyage in the Caribbean before returning to England. The ship Dampier was aboard had not left the coast of Jamaica when they came across a buccaneer band under the command of Bartholomew Sharpe and all the crew deserted to join the band. Dampier was left alone with the owner of the vessel, and after three or four days was persuaded to join the buccaneers himself.

The buccaneer crew sailed first for Porto Bello, which city they sacked, then decided to emulate the famous Henry Morgan by marching across the Isthmus of Panama to sack Panama City. They then planned to capture a ship at Panama and use it to attack Spanish settlements on the Pacific coast of South America, and finally to return through the Straits of Magellan.

The buccaneers managed to capture easily the small town of Santa Maria, midway across the Isthmus, but finding it completely devoid of anything of value they pressed on towards the Pacific. When they reached the coast the buccaneers had little difficulty in capturing a ship and a number of canoes, in which they sailed towards Panama. When they arrived off the city they found a squadron of eight Spanish men-of-war. Sharpe had taken his ship off to chase another prize, but the rest of the buccaneers under Captain Coxon fought the ships from their canoes. The marksmanship and the desperation of the buccaneers combined to give them victory, and by the end of the action five Spanish ships had been captured. The Buccaneer losses were heavy however, and the buccaneers were forced to abandon their hopes of taking Panama. Shortly afterwards disagreement broke out amongst the buccaneer band and forty-seven elected not to pursue the voyage further, but to return across the Isthmus. William Dampier was among this group, commanded by Captain John Cook. Upon reaching the Caribbean coast the buccaneers joined with another squadron of English and French ships, but quickly tired of their company. About twenty, including Dampier, parted company from the rest and sailed to Virginia[15].

While in Virginia Dampier met with John Cook once again and in August 1683 was persuaded to join him, along with some other veterans of Sharpe's expedition, on another voyage to the Pacific. They sailed from Virginia in a small ship called the *Revenge*, and shaped their course for the coast of Africa. At the Cape Verde Islands the buccaneers replenished their provisions, but shrank from taking a well -armed Dutch East Indiaman. They next sailed to the Guinea coast, and off Sierra Leone were able to capture a Danish ship of forty guns which was better suited to their purpose than the *Revenge*. They renamed their new ship the *Bachelor's Delight*, and exchanged the *Revenge* further down the coast for sixty young black women. Both ships had been well stocked with supplies and the buccaneers loaded the supplies from the *Revenge* into the *Bachelor's Delight* and set sail for Cape Horn.

In mid–February the buccaneers reached the latitude of Cape Horn, and on the 14 of that month a terrible storm blew up. One of Dampier's colleagues on this voyage was the scientist Ambrose Cowley who described the occasion:

We choosing of Valentines and discoursing of the intrigues of women there arose a prodigious storm, which did continue til the last day of the month … so that we concluded the discoursing of women at sea was very unlucky and occasioned the storm.

During the storm the *Bachelor's Delight* was blown south, and the navigators aboard reckoned her position to be sixty degrees and thirty minutes south, the furthest south that anyone had ever sailed up to that time. In early March the wind veered and the buccaneers were able to enter the Pacific. On the 19 March they spotted their first prize. Dampier wrote:

> We saw a ship to the southward of us coming with all the sail she could make after us. We lay muzzled to let her come up with us, for we supposed her to be a Spanish ship come from Valdivia bound to Lima; we being now to the northward of Valdivia, and this being the time of the year when ships that trade thence to Valdivia return home. They had the same opinion of us, and therefore made sure to take us, but coming nearer we both found our mistakes

This newcomer was the *Nicholas*, commanded by one John Eaton, who had travelled to the Pacific for the same purpose of plunder as the men of the *Bachelor's Delight*. The *Nicholas* too had been caught in the Valentine's Day storm, and had lost contact with a third English ship, the *Cygnet*, commanded by Captain Swan. The two ships sailed together for the island of Juan Fernandez.

Dampier and some of the other buccaneers had visited Juan Fernandez in 1681 when they had been in Sharpe's force. On that occasion they had been forced to flee from the island by the arrival of three Spanish ships, and had left one of their number behind, a Mosquito Indian named William. Dampier's account of the voyage describes in detail how William had survived on the island for three years. He had managed to notch his knife into a saw blade and had used it to cut up the barrel of his musket. These pieces of metal he had forged into harpoon heads and fishing hooks with which he had hunted goats, fish and seals. On the day of the English arrival William killed three goats and cooked them with cabbages before going down to the landing beach to welcome his old friends.

After sixteen days on Juan Fernandez the buccaneers set sail once more to the northward. In early May they took a small prize and held a council of war to decide their next move. It was decided that they would sail for Cape Blanco, south of Panama, and there wait for the Spanish treasure fleet sailing up the coast. Scurvy broke out and the two ships were forced to seek an anchorage at the island of Lobos, in the vicinity of Cape Blanco. A second council of war decided that their next enterprise should be to attack the town of Truxillo, but as the buccaneers were about to set sail they spied three ships. The three ships were easily captured and the buccaneers supplied themselves with flour, fruit, and quince marmalade. There was no gold to speak of aboard, but the buccaneers were also able to acquire news of Captain Swan, who had not been heard of since parting company from the *Nicholas* in February, three months earlier.

Swan was not a buccaneer, though he had earlier been one of Henry Morgan's band. On this occasion he had come into the Pacific with peaceful intentions, and funded by a consortium of London merchants hoped to open trade with the Spanish of South America. Since the days of Hawkins and Drake the Spanish colonists had been forbidden to trade with the English, and why Swan thought he alone might change their minds is a mystery. At Valdivia he went ashore and directly attempted to enter into trade negotiations with the authorities. Naturally, these attempts were unsuccessful, and only served to alert the Spanish to the presence of English pirates on the coast. One of the ships intercepted by the buccaneers off Lobos had been carrying 800,000 pieces of eight, but had been unloaded of this haul once the presence of the pirates was known of. Also as a result of Swan's blundering the Spanish at Truxillo were reported to be building a fort, which would make that town almost impossible for the buccaneers to capture with their meagre force.

With this news it was decided to abandon any attempt on Spanish settlements for the time being, and instead to establish themselves a base from which they could operate. They needed to rest their sick and wounded, replenish their stores, build up a supply of extra stores which could be hoarded for future use, and most importantly they needed to lay low for a few months in the hope the Spanish would think they had left the Pacific. The decision was made to sail for the Galapagos Islands.

Throughout his life Dampier's actions were largely dictated by his financial situation, and he stepped from one enterprise to the next in search of enough money to enjoy his Dorset estate. However, his great love and driving passion was naturalism, and the Galapagos Islands offered him such a scope as he had never seen before. His description of the giant turtles of the islands is almost as long as his description of the voyage there from Juan Fernandez, and remained the most popular in print for at least a century. He also dedicated time and paper to the description of the flora and other fauna of the islands. Dampier's shipmate Cowley also made his mark on the history of the Galapagos by giving several of them names which they still bear today. King Charles Island in honour of the monarch, York, Norfolk, and Albemarle named after dukes, Brattle, Crossman, Eure, and Bindloss were named after members of the buccaneer band, and one small island even bears the name Cowley's Island.

The buccaneers did not remain long in the Galapagos Islands however. Instead of replenishing and lying low as they had planned they became tempted by one of their Indian captives' descriptions of the riches and weakness of Rio Lexa. On the way back to the mainland John Cook died of a mysterious illness from which he had suffered since before their stay at Juan Fernandez. Cook was replaced by Edward Davis, and his body was taken ashore for burial. Three local natives arrived to watch Cook's funeral and started to ask 'many silly questions'. The buccaneers took the natives prisoner for fear they would divulge their presence to the Spaniards. One of the natives managed to escape and did exactly that, so that by the time the buccaneers arrived at the town defences had been organised and valuables had been spirited away to safety.

After six months cruising together in the Pacific the buccaneers had almost nothing to show for it. An attempt to employ natives to help with the cleaning of their ships ended in disaster and the parties began to quarrel. In September 1684 the two ships parted company. Within weeks the *Bachelor's Delight* had met with two other buccaneer vessels, one commanded by Peter Harris who had been an officer in Sharpe's expedition, the other the *Cygnet*. Captain Swan had been forced to turn buccaneer by the desertion of his men to Harris, and had been allowed to keep command of his ship. Within a short time several other buccaneer groups joined this band and so in the early months of 1685 Edward Davis found himself in command of a sizeable force of ten vessels and several hundred buccaneers. Once again, they set their sights on Panama.

This attack on Panama was thwarted, as the last had been, by the presence of a powerful Spanish squadron. Dissent among the buccaneers and the possible desertion of one of the French vessels allowed the Spanish to end the battle in control of the entrance to Panama harbour. The buccaneers next headed for the town of Leon, which they managed to take with some ease. Unfortunately all the Spanish troops had been withdrawn from the town in order to regroup for a counter attack, and the buccaneers were forced to leave empty handed. Shortly after this debacle the buccaneer band once more fell to quarrelling and each group went their own way. Dampier joined with Captain Swan in the *Cygnet*, for the naturalist in him wanted to see the northern part of America, and to cross the Pacific, both of which were part of Swan's plan.

After unsuccessful attempts to capture a gold ship in Acapulco harbour, the Manila galleon and the town of Santa Pecaque, Dampier was able to persuade Swan and the rest of the crew to set out across the Pacific. At the end of March 1686 they set out to cross the ocean in two vessels, and fifty-one days later the made the island of Guam. Food had been short on the voyage, and the men strictly rationed. From the outset the lack of food for such a long journey had been the men's principal worry, and they had determined to kill Captain Swan for food if their supplies ran out. When Swan had been eaten they were to kill all those who had supported the idea of a journey across the Pacific, including Dampier. They arrived at Guam with three days' food left. 'Ah, Dampier!' said Captain Swan on their arrival, 'you would have made them but a poor meal'. Dampier 'was as lean as the captain was lusty and fleshy'.

At Guam the buccaneers supplied themselves with food and water, and when they discovered they had once again missed their chance to capture the fabled Manila Galleon they agreed to sail on to the Philippines. At Mindanao Swan went ashore to negotiate for further supplies while the rest of the buccaneers received a hospitable welcome. In a few weeks the liquor sellers and prostitutes of Mindanao had relieved the buccaneers of all the treasure they had amassed. The subsequent restlessness brought about a mutiny, at the end of which Captain Swan was left at Mindanao with about three dozen others as the mutineers sailed away.

The mutiny was led by John Reed, a Bristol man, with whom Dampier could not get on, and there is some speculation as to why Dampier did not remain behind with his friend Captain Swan. It was January 1687 when the mutineers left Swan, and for almost a year they cruised about among the Spice Islands before sailing south and landing in Australia. In January 1688 they left Australia and Dampier begged to be allowed to leave the company at the next opportunity. It was not until May that Dampier and three others were allowed ashore with their sea chests. For the next two years Dampier engaged in several trading voyages in the Indian Ocean before he joined and East India Company convoy and arrived in England in 1691. He had not seen his wife or home for nearly twelve years, but he had circumnavigated the globe, still an incredible achievement 180 years after Magellan. He had no wealth to speak of, and his only possessions were his journal, sealed in a hollow bamboo, and a young Malay boy named Prince Jeoly, whom he was forced to sell.

Little is known of Dampier's life over the next few years. In 1697 he published the story of his circumnavigation under the title *A New Voyage Round the World*, a book which has delighted readers for three centuries. In August the following year John Evelyn the diarist records dining with Dampier at the house of the other great diarist of the age, Samuel Pepys. Evelyn wrote that Dampier had been appointed to the command of a Royal Navy ship, the *Roebuck*, and in this vessel he sailed once more for Australia in January 1699[16].

The voyage of the *Roebuck* could hardly have been called a success by anyone's standards, and in fact the ship was lost near Ascension Island. Dampier and the crew were marooned for over a month until a passing East India Company convoy picked them up and returned them to England. Dampier never again enjoyed command of a Royal Navy vessel, but in 1703 was appointed to command an expedition of two ships, privately financed by a consortium of merchants, to act as privateers in the Pacific.

The expedition was blighted from the start, possibly because of Dampier's nature, when one of the ships set sail without the other. Dampier was left behind in the twenty-six-gun *St. George* while his consort ship sailed off on her own account. Dampier's delay was caused by his refusal to set sail without the owners' agent, who was in fact an old friend of Dampier's from their days together on the *Cygnet*. Dampier had persuaded the owners to employ this man, Edward Morgan, to look after their interests during the voyage, but at the time set for departure Morgan was in prison and Dampier had to wait for his release. The *St. George* finally sailed from Bristol at the end of April 1703, and set course for Kinsale in Ireland. Dampier spent four months refitting in Ireland, but during that time joined forces with another ship, the *Cinque Ports*, and finally set off in September 1703.

At the Cape Verde Islands Dampier quarrelled with the first lieutenant and the latter was put ashore with his sea chest and a servant. When the ships reached Brazil a short while later Dampier quarrelled with the new first lieutenant, and he too went ashore, along with eight others. Captain Pickering of the *Cinque Ports* died and was replaced by the lieutenant of that ship, Thomas Stradling. In January 1704 the two ships reached Cape Horn and sailed into the Pacific. Almost immediately they were separated by bad weather, but in early February rendezvoused at Juan Fernandez.

After three weeks on Juan Fernandez, a ship was sighted and such was the haste to get to sea to chase her that five men and most of the stockpiled supplies were abandoned. After a chase which lasted through the night the buccaneers caught up the ship, which proved to be a French ship of 400 tons, and lay alongside her exchanging broadsides. After seven hours fighting a storm blew up and enabled the French ship to get away. The buccaneers returned to Juan Fernandez and the French ship sailed for Lima to spread the news of another English expedition into the Pacific.

On their return to Juan Fernandez the buccaneers found that two more powerful French ships were riding in the harbour, preventing their collection of invaluable stores, and their boats. The buccaneers sailed to the mainland and contemplated an attack on Arica, but without boats were unable to land. A few days later they came across two ships and set sails to overhaul them. When they came up with the two ships one of them turned out to be the French ship they had chased from Juan Fernandez, while the other was one of the ships which had been waiting there on their return. It was a golden opportunity to prevent news of their presence reaching the Spanish, but Dampier vacillated and the two ships got safely to Lima. The following day the buccaneers captured a Spanish ship, which Dampier allowed to go without plundering much of her cargo. Dampier's reason, or so he told his men, was that he did not want to load their ships up with stolen cargoes when they could load them with gold and silver as soon as they made a successful attack on a Spanish treasure-handling settlement. When, a few days later, the buccaneers captured another ship richly laden, which Dampier again allowed to go after taking little of value the crews of both ships began to grow restless.

After a short time spent in the Galapagos Islands Dampier and Stradling led an attack on Santa Maria, which Dampier had known on his voyage with Sharpe. A series of blunders and mishaps meant that the Spanish in Santa Maria had two full days warning of Dampier's approach. When several of the buccaneers were killed in an ambush Dampier gave up the attempt on the town, expecting to find it empty as Sharpe's men had. Dampier's men were once again despondent, but on the night of their return to their ships a Spanish merchantman unwittingly sailed alongside them and was captured without a shot being fired.

While the buccaneers were plundering this prize at their leisure discontent once again broke out, and Dampier and Stradling began to quarrel. At length the two ships separated, and the Cinque Ports sailed to Juan Fernandez to collect the men and stores that were left there. The stores had all been taken by the French ships, and three of the five men had been killed, but two survivors guided the ship into a safe anchorage and the crew set about a long overdue refit. The sailing master of the *Cinque Ports*, Alexander Selkirk, felt that the ship was unseaworthy and refused to sail in her. Expecting Dampier to arrive at the island he voluntarily marooned himself there when Stradling set sail again. Selkirk's assessment of the state of the Cinque Ports was accurate, a short while later she was wrecked and most of the crew drowned. Stradling himself managed to get ashore with half a dozen others, but was captured by the Spanish and spent some time in prison, eventually ending up in Normandy, from whence he managed to escape and return to England, where he stood trial for his actions in the Pacific.

Dampier meanwhile sailed down the coast of Peru, taking some insignificant prizes and engaging in an inconclusive battle with a Spanish man-of-war. A small ship was taken and renamed the *Dragon*, but one of Dampier's officers named John Clipperton led a mutiny and sailed off in her with twenty-one men and various supplies. The men remaining under Dampier's command then continued to cruise off the coast of Mexico, taking prizes and waiting for the Manila Galleon taking gold to the East Indies. So often before Dampier had been part of a scheme to take this ship, laden with fabled riches, and so often had those schemes failed, usually without the Manila Galleon even being sighted. Eventually though the patience of the buccaneers was rewarded and the Manila Galleon hove into view. There was great excitement aboard the *St. George*, and one of their prisoners suggested that the buccaneers should board the galleon before the Spanish could run out their big guns. What actually happened next is obscured by the fact that three entirely different versions of the same events survive. What we do know is that the buccaneers failed to board the Manila Galleon and forever missed their chance to do so.

Mutiny once again spread throughout the *St. George*, and six weeks later came to a head. It is difficult to say who was the mutinous party, for thirty-three men refused to go any further with Dampier in command, but Dampier and his supporters decided to break with their employers and go off on their own account, effectively as pirates. The thirty-three were led by Dampier's friend Edward Morgan, and transferred themselves to another prize which had been renamed *Dragon*. The share of the profits deemed to be the owners' was placed in the *Dragon*, along with supplies and four guns. In February 1705 the two ships separated and Dampier, with his twenty-seven men landed to raid the tiny town of Puna. A few days later they captured a Spanish ship and left the leaking *St. George*.

Dampier decided once more to sail across the Pacific, but on arrival in the Dutch East Indies disaster struck. Unknown to Dampier, John Clipperton had stolen the letter of marque which legalised Dampier's activities. Dampier had not noticed the loss, but now was required to show it to prove that he and his men were not pirates. Unable to do so they were all thrown into prison. All the sources which describe Dampier's expedition, and the journeys of some of those who broke away from him, are silent on what happened to Dampier and his men after their imprisonment. Even how Dampier managed to get out of prison is not known, and in fact nothing is known for certain until his return to England in late 1707. Once again Dampier had circumnavigated the globe, but once more he was impoverished and without immediate prospects.

The controversy which raged over Dampier's handling of the expedition was fuelled by the appearance of three different accounts of the voyage. The first, written by William Funnell, a junior officer of Dampier's, lays the blame for most of the misfortunes encountered firmly at Dampier's feet. The second account was written by Dampier himself in response to Funnell's, and tells a very different story in which the drunkenness of the crew and the insubordination of the junior officers are blamed. The third account was written by Midshipman Welbe, and holds Dampier responsible for the failures of the voyage, but does not necessarily agree with Funnell's account in the details. Because of these three accounts all being in print at the same time Dampier's reputation was not as damaged as might be imagined, and within a few months he found himself employment as pilot (navigator) to another privateering enterprise being financed and fitted out in Bristol.

The £13,000 cost of fitting out two ships, the *Duke* and *Duchess*, was met by a group of merchants including Sir John Hawkins and Francis Rogers, both descendants of their more famous sixteenth-century namesakes. The ships were to carry twice the usual number of officers as a precaution against mutiny, evidently lessons had been learned from Dampier's last voyage. In overall command was Woodes Rogers of Bristol, a relative of Francis Rogers, and probably the best man for the job. The *Duke* was fitted with thirty guns, the *Duchess* with twenty-six, and they left Bristol at the beginning of August 1708. A month later the ships left Cork harbour, having put in there to recruit more men and collect more supplies.

Only a few days into the voyage the first mutiny broke out. The extra officers on board may have been effective, for the ringleaders were swiftly rounded up. Rogers then had the chief amongst them flogged by the other mutineers, correctly believing that this would encourage the breaking up of 'unlawful friendships'. Rogers had perhaps spoken with Dampier about the difficulties of his previous voyage, was almost certainly aware of the mutinies he had faced, and was determined not to suffer a similar fate. Unlike previous privateers on voyages of plunder, Rogers was determined to keep discipline, and to operate at all times within the rules set down for the expedition.

In early January 1709 the *Duke* and *Duchess* rounded Cape Horn and made straight to Juan Fernandez, reaching that island before the end of the month. The two ships were unable to approach the island because of contrary winds and falling night, but Rogers sent a boat ashore for fresh water. Suddenly a light appeared in the harbour. Rogers fired a gun to recall the boat and placed lights in the rigging so that the boat crew would be able to find their way back to the ships. It was decided that the light was probably from French ships, and that the following day they would have to fight them, or die of thirst. The following morning the boat was sent ahead once again, but did not return. The ships cleared for action and Rogers sent a larger boat, the pinnace, to see what had become of the first boat. A short while later the pinnace returned with 'an abundance of crawfish, with a man clothed in goatskins, who looked wilder than the first owners of them'. After four years and four months Alexander Selkirk, left behind by Captain Stradling, was rescued.

When Selkirk saw Dampier was aboard this new expedition he refused to remain aboard and said he would rather remain on the island than sail under his command. Only when other members of the crew assured Selkirk that Dampier was not in command did he agree to join them. Dampier, for his part, testified to Selkirk's skill as a seaman, and Rogers employed Selkirk as a master's mate of the Duke. Selkirk showed his new companions over Juan Fernandez, showed them the places to get water and meat. After two weeks they set sail once more, for the Islands of Lobos.

At Lobos the ships were cleaned and two small prizes they had taken and renamed *Beginning* and *Increase* were fitted with guns. The increase was placed under the command of Selkirk. Rogers' next intention was to capture the town of Guayacil and hold it to ransom. The seamen felt that they had not signed on for operations ashore, and that it was a more dangerous plan than they were expected to undertake. Rogers altered the rules of plunder, allowing the men to take items which had previously been forbidden such as bedding, clothes, gold rings, buttons, liquor, silver or gold crucifixes, and gold or silver watches. The men were still forbidden to steal money, precious stones, or ladies' earrings from individuals, but they agreed to the attacking of Guayacil.

The town of Guayacil lay a little up-river from the coast, so Rogers and his men had first to take the village of Puna, at the mouth of the river. Dampier had captured Puna on his previous voyage, and the buccaneers found it easy to do so a second time. It took at least two days for the buccaneers to make their way in their boats against a strong current, and by the time they arrived at Guayacil the inhabitants were already preparing a strong defence. Instead of trying to assault the town Rogers now sent a messenger with a flag of truce to offer an ultimatum to the inhabitants. If they did not buy from him the slaves he had captured Rogers would capture and burn their town. In addition to a fair price for his slaves Rogers also demanded a ransom to prevent him burning the town and ships in harbour anyway. The Spanish eventually agreed and Rogers' men took possession of the town. Most of the wealthy inhabitants had taken themselves and their valuables to their country homes, further up river. A party of men were sent to search these homes, and came back with a considerable store of loot which had been taken from the Spanish ladies.

Rogers and his men returned to Puna to await the payment of the ransom. When it finally arrived the ransom was less than Rogers had demanded, but he was anxious to be away from Guayacil so accepted the money, freed his hostages, and sailed for the Galapagos Islands. Before they reached those islands though, the crews of the Duke and Duchess began to suffer a terrible disease and a number of them died. A prisoner taken at Guayacil told them that shortly before their arrival a terrible plague had swept the town, and many had died. So many had died that they were buried in a mass grave beneath the church that Rogers and his men had used as a headquarters. At first they could find no fresh water in the Galapagos and the deaths continued. Eventually water was found and the health of the survivors restored. Another prize they had taken was renamed *Marquis* and fitted out to join the squadron. When they had sorted through their accumulated loot the buccaneers abandoned the *Beginning* and *Increase*, and set their course for the Bay of Panama.

After taking a few prizes in the bay the buccaneers returned to the Galapagos Islands to stock up on giant turtles, then sailed for Cape St Lucas to wait for the Manila Galleon. On 21 December 1709 a ship was sighted and the *Duke* and *Duchess* gave chase. As the wind died down both ships sent boats to investigate the stranger, unsure whether it was the *Marquis* or the Manila Galleon. Finally it became clear that they were following the Manila Galleon, but the wind prevented them from catching her up. Through the night the two English boats followed the Spanish ship, with lights burning so that the *Duke* and *Duchess* could follow them. The following day the wind was sufficient for the *Duke* and *Duchess* to close the gap. The Duke drew alongside and fired several broadsides into the Spanish ship, then edged ahead and turning, fired a broadside into her bow. By the time the *Duchess* arrived the Spanish ship had surrendered. Interrogation of her officers revealed that the prize was indeed a richly laden ship returning from Manila, but that she was only the companion to a larger, richer ship.

Rogers himself had been wounded in the fighting, part of his jaw was shot away, but the arrival of the *Marquis* enabled him to take the battered *Duke* into harbour and send the other two ships out to patrol for the larger Manila Galleon. On Boxing Day Rogers' lookouts reported that the *Duchess* and *Marquis* were sailing in company with a third ship. Immediately the *Duke* was put to sea, but the other two ships began the engagement with the heavily armed Manila Galleon before Rogers could reach them. By the time the Duke reached the other ships the *Marquis* and *Duchess* had been badly beaten by the larger guns of the Spanish ship. The *Duke* joined the battle, but her small guns made no impression on the thick timbers of the Spaniard, and when Rogers received a second wound all three English ships broke off the fight.

In early January the buccaneers set sail across the Pacific for Guam, arriving there two months later. From Guam they sailed to the Dutch held Batavia (now Jakarta), where they sold the *Marquis*. The ships waited three months at the Cape of Good Hope for a convoy to see them safely home, and they dropped anchor in the Thames in October 1711.

Dampier died in 1715, still owed most of his wages from his third and final circumnavigation. Selkirk's story was published, and inspired Daniel Defoe to write *Robinson Crusoe*. Bristol legend states that Selkirk and Defoe met in Bristol, but it is unlikely, and certainly unproven. Most of the other people involved in the voyage disappeared into obscurity, except perhaps for the self styled 'Captain of Marines'. Dr Thomas Dover was one of the investors in the voyage and travelled aboard the *Duke* to oversee the investors' interests. Although he was a successful practitioner in Bristol Dr Dover preferred to revel in his chosen title throughout the voyage, but had a very successful career in later years, earning the nickname 'Dr Quicksilver' for his prescription of mercury in large quantities. Woodes Rogers published his account of the voyage and we shall meet him again in a later chapter.

8

THE PIRATE ROUND

As the Spanish defence of their possessions in the New World
became stronger, in direct response to the activities of the buccaneers, so the pirates and privateers of Europe and the Americas
started to seek new hunting grounds. The Indian Ocean and the
Red Sea became favourite areas for the pirates to operate in, and
the circular trade between the eastern waters and the Americas or
Europe became known as the 'pirate round'. Although English and
American pirates had been working in the Indian Ocean and Red
Sea since the early seventeenth century it was not until the 1690s
that the pirate round became properly established. So effective
were the pirates in these water that they drew too much adverse
attention to themselves, and by the opening years of the eighteenth century the heyday of the pirate round was over. This end
was probably brought about by a combination of factors, the most

important of which were the influence of the East India Company, and the outbreak of the War of the Spanish Succession. The East India Company's monopolies were endangered by the actions of the pirates, and they were successful at bringing pressure to bear in various quarters for the suppression of the pirates. The War of the Spanish Succession (sometimes called Queen Anne's War) meant that the number of Royal Navy ships and privateers at sea increased dramatically, and there was enough legitimate employment for the sea dogs to prevent their needing to resort to piracy.

Not all of the pirates involved in the plundering of Arab and Indian ships based themselves in America. From the beginning of the pirate round Madagascar had been used as a base by pirates. The most famous of the pirates who used Madagascar in the heyday of the pirate round was one of the most successful pirates of all time. His career was short, but he managed to capture two fabulous prizes before disappearing into obscurity with his riches. Though he is largely forgotten now, he was, in his own time, known as the 'Arch Pirate', and had plays and books written about him. His name was Henry Avery and he was born in Plymouth.

Little is known about Avery's early life, reliable records just do not exist to describe his birth and upbringing, but his contemporaries had him born in Plymouth in 1653, the son of John Avery, an innkeeper. John Avery wanted his son to become a scholar, but young Henry had no time for learning and 'became vicious and could swear to any point of the compass'. As a young lad Henry went to sea and eventually joined the Royal Navy and served aboard HMS *Rupert* and HMS *Albemarle* as a midshipman. In 1694 Avery was mate aboard a Bristol privateer, the *Charles the Second*, sailing to Corunna.

From Corunna the *Charles the Second* was to sail to the West Indies, but instead waited for several months, the crew growing more restless by the day. Eventually a group of men, including some from another ship also waiting at Corunna, led by Avery, took over the ship and got her underway. The captain had been sick and was asleep in his cabin when Avery and the mutineers set to work, but quickly awoke and demanded to know what was going on. When Avery informed the captain of the mutinous seizure of the ship the captain elected to be put into a boat with five or six others, to make their way to land.

The pirates renamed their ship the *Fancy*, and sailed south. At the Cape Verde Islands they took three English ships, and two Danish ships at the Island of Principe. They then rounded the Cape of Good Hope and made for Madagascar. At Madagascar, Avery loaded supplies and some extra guns aboard the *Fancy*, and joined forces with some other pirates he found there. Now with three ships, the *Fancy*, *Pearl*, and *Portsmouth Adventure*, Avery set sail for the mouth of the Red Sea, where he was joined by a fourth ship, the *Amity*, commanded by another noted pirate rounder, Thomas Tew.

With a formidable squadron now under his command Avery felt strong enough to attack the Pilgrim convoy which sailed across the Red Sea between India and the Middle East. As well as many wealthy personages travelling on pilgrimages the convoy also carried merchants and their wares. The convoy was as rich and as tempting a target as the Spanish plate fleets of Drake's day, or the Manila ships of Dampier's. Most of the Pilgrim fleet managed to slip past Avery's squadron, but after days of waiting the pirates finally spotted an Indian ship, the *Fateh Mahomed*.

The pirates gave chase to the *Fateh Mahomed* and after a short fight she was captured. On board the pirates found gold and silver worth £50,000, but Thomas Tew had been killed during the fight and the crew of the *Amity* broke away from the pirate band at around this time. The treasure was shared out amongst the men and the remaining ships waited for another Pilgrim ship. Within a few days they spotted a ship, much larger that the *Fateh Mahomed* and gave chase.

This new ship, the *Gang-I-Sawai*, carried sixty two guns, had a large crew and was owned by the Great Mogul himself. Although Avery's forty-six gun *Fancy* was big for a pirate ship it would have been no match for the *Gang-I-Sawai* without the support of the two sloops. Avery began a long range artillery duel with the Indian ship, attempting to disable her so that she could be pounded and attacked at the pirates' leisure. One of Avery's first shots damaged the main mast of the *Gang-I-Sawai*, and one of the Indian cannons blew up on deck, but still the fight continued. The two sloops used the time to manoeuvre themselves into the best positions for boarding, and after two hours fighting the first of the pirates swarmed aboard from the sloops, one at each end of the prize. The defenders were caught between two sets of pirates when the *Fancy* came up and Avery's men joined the fight. So desperate were the defenders that a number of Arab women were dressed as men and made to fight.

What followed was an orgy of violence, torture, rape and theft. An elderly relative of the Great Mogul was raped, along with her servants and any other female passengers. One man killed himself, his wife, and their nurse to escape being made to watch them raped. Others threw themselves overboard to escape the depravity, and a number of women are recorded as having been treated so roughly that they died of the experience. Men were tortured until they revealed the whereabouts of their treasure, and anyone who resisted was slaughtered. The ships lay becalmed and the looting and ravishing lasted several days.

When the ships finally did part the pirates had made one of the largest hauls in history. In coin alone it was estimated that each man's share was £1,000, the equivalent of nearly sixty years' wages for an able seaman of the time. The total sum when all the other goods, jewels and uncoined gold and silver are included is unimaginable. Avery and his two consorts sailed for Madagascar planning to lay up some of their gold there and build themselves a fort and settlement. It struck Avery though that perhaps the gold would be safer if it were all aboard his ship, so he summoned the other captains to explain his idea to them.

Neither of their ships, he explained, was strong enough to resist capture by an enemy of any force if they were separated. Nor were either of them as seaworthy as the *Fancy*. Would it not be sensible, he asked, for all the treasure to be moved aboard the *Fancy* for safekeeping until they reached Madagascar? Incredibly the other captains agreed. Avery's arguments made good sense, and by sealing each chest of treasure with three seals it would be impossible for Avery or his men to tamper with the treasure without their knowing about it. Accordingly, all the plunder from the *Fateh Mahomed* and the *Gang-I-Sawai* were moved aboard the *Fancy*.

For two days the ships sailed together, but on the morning of the third day the men aboard the sloops awoke to realise that the *Fancy* had left them during the night. The weather had been fair, and they had all agreed the course, so the only explanation was treachery. Avery had called his men together and tempted them into deserting their comrades, so keeping a greater portion of treasure for themselves. Avery wanted to end his life of piracy while he were rich and alive, and persuaded his men to do likewise.

They sailed first for Providence in the Bahamas, where an enormous bribe to the governor assured their safety. Here the pirate band split up. Avery and some of his men sold the *Fancy* and bought themselves a sloop in which they sailed to New England. More of the crew left the band at Boston, while Avery sailed for Ireland with twenty or more. Some of the men who left the ship at Boston or the Bahamas succeeded in obtaining pardons or in making their way into obscure but respectable society. Six of the men who had sailed to Ireland, and then made their way to England, were captured and hanged. The men Avery had left behind in the sloops were forced to settle on Madagascar, since they had no supplies fit for a long voyage.

What happened to Avery himself is obscure. After landing in Co. Donegal, Avery disappears from records. Some stories suggest that he went to sea once more and ended up living on a paradise island, but that is probably fantasy. Captain Charles Johnson, in his *General History of the Robberies and Murders of the Most Notorious Pirates*[17], suggests that Avery went from Ireland to Bideford where he settled down under an assumed name. He travelled to Bristol to try to sell some of his diamonds, but the Bristol merchants threatened instead to expose him and he was forced to flee to Ireland, leaving his diamonds in their possession. He continued to pester the merchants, but was consistently refused and ended up a beggar. He was able to work a passage from Ireland to Plymouth, and then travelled overland to Bideford, where he died and was buried in a pauper's grave. There is nothing inherently unlikely about this story and it may well be true, certainly Johnson seems to have had access to information not available to others. On the other hand it may be a fictional ending, inserted by Johnson to provide a moral element to the story of the arch pirate. In fact, there is no good evidence concerning Avery's last years and demise, so we are free to believe what we wish.

Another West Country man, Robert Culliford of Looe, made his name in the Indian Ocean in the 1690s, but is best remembered now for his association with the notorious Captain Kidd[18]. Culliford first met Kidd when they served together aboard a privateer in the West Indies in the late 1680s. In 1689 Kidd was placed in command of a prize crew, of which Culliford was a member, in a French ship they had captured. The prize was sailed to Nevis where she was renamed the *Blessed William* and put under Kidd's command as a privateer. Straightaway the *Blessed William* joined a Royal Navy squadron for an attack on a French settlement which led to considerable profit for those involved.

Some months later the *Blessed William* was ordered to join another Royal Navy squadron, this time hunting down a squadron of French ships. The crew argued that by involving themselves in a sea battle they were putting themselves to great risk, with little hope of any profit or plunder at the end of it. Kidd refused to listen to the crew, but while he was ashore on Nevis mutiny broke out. Opinion is divided over whether Culliford or one William May was the ringleader of the mutiny, but the *Blessed William* was sailed away by the mutineers and May was elected the new captain.

At the end of 1690 the *Blessed William* sailed for Madagascar to embark on a piratical cruise. Culliford and May left the ship at the Nicobar Islands and returned to New York, perhaps trying to distance themselves from the mutiny and subsequent piracy. In around early 1694 May and Culliford joined the crew of the New York ship *Pearl*, May as captain and Culliford as gunner. The *Pearl* was one of the ships that was to be companion to Avery at the taking of the *Gang-I-Sawai*. The next few incidents in Culliford's life are difficult to untangle, and conflicting reports make it almost impossible to reliably reconstruct the sequence of events which led to Culliford's reunion with Kidd three years later.

At some time shortly after the capture of the *Gang-I-Sawai* Culliford was aboard the merchantman *Josiah* as a gunner. It seems likely that Culliford led a mutiny, or was at least involved with it, on board the *Josiah*, somewhere near Madras. A short while later some loyal members of the crew retook the ship and Culliford was marooned with some of his co-conspirators on the Nicobar Islands. In 1696 Culliford and his companions were rescued by the crew of the former East India Company ship the *Mocha Frigate*.

Almost immediately after leaving port a number of the *Mocha's* crew, led by one Ralph Stout, mutinied and seized the ship. The captain was murdered, and those members of the crew that had not fled embarked on a career of piracy. When Culliford and his companions boarded the *Mocha* they eagerly joined the crew, and Culliford appears to have held a position of some rank. In 1697 Stout was killed, possibly by his own men, and Culliford was elected captain of the *Mocha*. At around this time the Mocha was renamed the *Resolution*.

In the region of the Spice Islands one of the pirate lookouts spotted an English merchant ship, the *Dorill*, belonging to the East India Company. Culliford's men crammed on extra sail to catch the *Dorill*, and hoisted a red flag to signify that no quarter would be given if the crew resisted. Despite the fact that the *Resolution* was only half the size of the *Dorill*, the pirates hoped that their reputation and the threat of no mercy would be enough to make the East Indiaman surrender. When the two ships came close the *Dorill* fired a broadside, which shattered the *Resolution's* mainmast. The pirates faltered and the *Dorill's* boldness won the day. Culliford retreated to St Mary's Island off Madagascar with his damaged ship, capturing a few smaller prizes on the way, and plundering a French ship in the harbour.

In May 1698, while the *Resolution* was anchored at St Mary's, undergoing repairs after the fight with the *Dorill*, Captain Kidd arrived with his ship, the *Adventure Galley*, and a prize, the *Quedah Merchant*. Kidd had been employed to hunt down pirates in the Indian Ocean, partly in response to the outcry over the depredations of men like Avery, Tew, and indeed Culliford. Kidd's commission also provided for him to capture or sink French ships that he came across. It was this last clause which gave Kidd an extremely dubious excuse to seize the *Quedah Merchant*, the captain of which was English, but who carried French passes (as well as passes of other nations). The *Quedah Merchant* had been carrying a rich cargo, and it was probably this which tempted Kidd to throw off the pretence of legitimacy.

Had Kidd still considered his commission valid he should have taken Culliford prisoner, along with his crew. It is difficult to understand why he did not, in view of the fact that this meeting with Culliford must have reminded him of the loss of his first command, the *Blessed William*, eight years previously. At his trial Kidd claimed that all but thirteen of his men had deserted to Culliford's crew, and in view of his overwhelming firepower and the fact that Culliford's ship was in the middle of repairs, it is unlikely that Kidd could have come up with any other plausible reason. There is probably an element of truth in Kidd's statement, at least as far as some of his men deserting to Culliford, but other evidence suggests that it was never Kidd's ambition to arrest Culliford and the two commanders spent some days in friendly revelry.

At this time Kidd had probably not determined his next course of action, but a number of his crew were keen to remain in the Indian Ocean, in the pursuit of more prizes. Culliford was known to be planning further expeditions and a number of Kidd's men joined his crew for that reason. Kidd apparently made Culliford a gift of some much needed supplies and some of his surplus guns. In June 1698 Culliford left St Mary's with a resupplied ship and a larger crew. Once more, the history of his activities becomes clouded by conflicting and incomplete reports.

In September 1698 Culliford joined forces with a Dutch pirate named Dirk Chivers, who had been aboard one of the sloops deserted by Avery. With Chivers' ship, the *Soldado*, and another ship called the *Pelican*, Culliford led an attack on the *Great Mohammed*. All three ships pursued the Arab merchantman, the *Resolution* firing shot after shot with her bowchasers (guns facing forward) and the two smaller vessels attempted to board. The *Soldado* reached the *Great Mohammed* first, and as her men climbed over the side of the merchantmen the Arab crew called out their surrender. By the time the *Pelican* arrived alongside, the battle was over.

The *Great Mohammed* was one of the largest ships taken by pirates in those waters to that date and contained a cargo worth £130,000. The crew of the *Pelican* were denied their shares in the prize, Culliford and Chivers claiming that they had not taken part in the battle. Chivers ship was, by this time, becoming unseaworthy, so he transferred himself and his crew to the much larger prize, which he renamed *New Soldado*. Captain Wheeler of the *Pelican* next set off on his own, while Culliford and Chivers remained in company together taking more prizes, and using St Mary's Island as a base.

In September 1699 Culliford, Chivers, Wheeler, and several other pirates were at anchor at St Mary's when a Royal Navy squadron appeared at the mouth of the harbour. Culliford and Chivers both sank their ships in the entrance to the harbour to prevent the British squadron from entering, but in fact the ships, under Commodore Warren, had come to offer a general amnesty to pirates who surrendered themselves.

Culliford took advantage of the offer of a pardon and returned to England. He had to stand trial, as a formality, to ensure he was eligible for a pardon, but was soon a free man. Ironically his trial took place on the same day as one of Captain Kidd's trials. Culliford received a pardon while Kidd was censured for colluding with a known pirate; Culliford. Culliford later testified as a prosecution witness against another pirate named Burgess, whom he had identified in London, but thereafter disappears from the records. It has been put forward that he may have joined the Royal Navy, and though the evidence is slim, it is quite possible that that is indeed the case.

With the end of the seventeenth century the heyday of the pirate round ended. A few European and American pirates remained in the Indian Ocean, using Madagascar as a base, but their fortunes were not so good as they had been in former years. One of these men was Thomas White, a Plymouth-born seaman who found himself stranded on Madagascar and who took part in several piratical voyages in an attempt to meet with a European ship on which he could return home. White even resorted to adding a deck to an open boat in the hope of putting to sea and meeting a passing merchantman. Eventually White took to the life of piracy for its own sake and made a steady succession of captures, occasionally changing one ship for a better one, until he and his men had made a sufficient sum. The divided their plunder and returned to Madagascar where White fell ill and died.

One of the last spates of piracy in the Indian Ocean by European and American pirates was led by Plymouth man Edmund Condent[19] in 1718. Condent was an officer aboard a New York merchant sloop sailing from the West Indies when, for reasons unknown, the crew decided to embark on a career of piracy. When they took their first prize the captain of the pirates and some of the crew decided to fit her out as a pirate ship, leaving Condent in command of the sloop.

After taking several prizes Condent sailed for the Cape Verde Islands where he plundered merchantmen at will and captured a Dutch privateer. Finding this last prize more suited to his purpose he abandoned his sloop and renamed the prize *Flying Dragon*. Once again Condent crossed the Atlantic and ravaged Portuguese shipping on the coast of Brazil. Here he captured the *Wright Galley*, commanded by fellow Plymouth man John Spelt. Condent treated Spelt with unusual courtesy, and retained his ship for some time. When they came across a Dutch merchantman Condent had a pirate flag hoisted in the *Wright Galley*, and the apparent threat of two pirate ships was enough to make the Dutch captain surrender.

Condent eventually sent Captain Spelt on his way with his ship and continued attacking ships up and down the coast of Brazil. At one point it is alleged that the *Flying Dragon* met a Portuguese man-of-war of seventy guns and engaged her for an hour-and-a-half before being forced to flee. Word also reached Condent that the crew of another pirate ship had been captured by the Portuguese and were being held in prison. All the Portuguese prisoners the pirates took were tortured to try to extract further information about the captured pirates. Ears and noses were cut off, and priests were ridden around the decks of the *Flying Dragon* for sport. A short while later the pirates set sail for Africa, where they took some prizes, and then round the Cape of Good Hope for Madagascar.

In the summer of 1719 the *Flying Dragon* arrived at St Mary's Island, and Condent's crew was supplemented by some men who had been part of a pirate crew left there seven or eight years previously. After some months of very profitable cruising Condent took an Arab ship, whose name is lost, containing a treasure valued by contemporaries at £150,000. Shortly after this prize was taken Condent and his men returned to St Mary's where the plunder was divided, leaving each man with a share of around £2,000. Here the crew of the *Flying Dragon* broke up. Some of the men elected to stay with Condent, and they sailed the *Flying Dragon* to Reunion Island to negotiate for a pardon from the French governor. Like Avery and Culliford, Condent's end is not clear. Captain Johnson would have us believe, in his *General History*, that Condent married the sister-in-law of the French governor then settled as a merchant in St Malo, Brittany. Alas, the historical evidence cannot support that theory, or any other.

9

THE GOLDEN AGE

In 1713 the Treaty of Utrecht was signed, ending the War of the Spanish Succession which had ravaged Europe and the colonies for a decade. With the end of the conflict navies were reduced to their peacetime establishments, and the opportunities for business-men and speculators to make profits from privateering dwindled. As a result thousands of seamen found themselves unemployed, with no course open to them but piracy. From around 1715 until the majority of pirates were suppressed around a decade later was the true Golden Age of Piracy.

One of the pirates who really epitomised the golden age was probably born in Hittisleigh on the northern edge of Dartmoor in around 1689. Little is known of Samuel Bellamy's early life, except that he was a seaman, and was probably one of those who were out of work after the Treaty of Utrecht. In 1715 he was in

New England when a terrible storm sank many vessels in the Gulf of Mexico. Among the vessels reported to have been sunk were Spanish treasure ships, carrying a fortune in gold and silver for anyone who could salvage it. Bellamy persuaded a New England jeweller named Williams to finance an expedition to try to salvage some of the sunken treasure, and Williams in fact joined the expedition.

When Bellamy and Williams reached the Caribbean they found that the sunken treasure would not be so easy to recover as they thought. The most accessible wrecks had either already been plundered or were guarded, the rest could not be reached with the diving technology of the early eighteenth century. Unwilling to lose their investment of time and money Bellamy and Williams turned to piracy. The two sloops, *Sultana* and *Mary-Anne*, they had provided themselves with for treasure hunting were ideal pirate vessels and they took a number of prizes in a short time. In February 1717 Bellamy and Williams captured the greatest prize of their careers.

The *Whydah* was a vessel of around 300 tons, built for speed and handiness. She had only been built in 1715, and was on her second voyage, from England with a cargo of trade goods, which were exchanged in Africa for slaves, who in turn were traded in the Americas for sugar, tobacco, gold and silver for the English market. Near the Bahamas the *Whydah* was chased by the *Sultana* and *Mary-Anne*, before being boarded by Bellamy's pirates. Once aboard her, Bellamy realised that the *Whydah* was an almost perfect pirate ship. She was small enough to be handled by a reasonable sized crew, could mount a powerful broadside, and above all, she was fast. The latter was an essential quality in pirate ships if they were to catch up with a fleeing prize, or escape from war ships themselves. Bellamy took the *Whydah* as his flagship, leaving the *Sultana* for those of the crew of the *Whydah* who declined to join the pirates.

Bellamy then sailed north and took a number of prizes off Virginia, but in early March a terrible storm blew up. The *Whydah* and *Mary-Anne* were forced to run before the storm, during which the *Whydah's* main and mizzenmasts were lost. A leak was sprung in the bow of the *Whydah* and she had to be continually pumped to prevent the water level in the hold rising. The waves broke over the stern of the ship, smashing the taff-rail and nearly sweeping the two men at the wheel overboard. On the fourth day the weather abated and the two ships were able to make contact. The *Mary-Anne* had also been blown about by the storm, but was not as badly damaged as the *Whydah*. The pirates set their course for Carolina to repair their ships, but the wind veered and they changed their destination to Rhode Island. The *Whydah's* carpenter found and plugged the leak, and jury masts were set up.

In early April the pirates took a sloop off South Carolina which they looted then sank. A week or two later they captured another sloop off Cape Cod which they added to their squadron. Somewhere in Maine the pirates went ashore and built a small fort to protect themselves while they emptied their ships and heeled them over to clean the bottoms, before continuing their journey north. Off Newfoundland the ships were separated by another storm. Bellamy spotted a ship and gave chase, but when the two ships came together Bellamy found that he had chased down a French man-of-war. The French ship had a heavier broadside than the *Whydah*, but the pirate nonetheless 'engaged with great resolution'.

For two hours the ships fired at each other, twice the French tried to board the *Whydah*, and twice they were repulsed. Broadside after broadside was fired, but Bellamy realised that the French ship was too powerful for him to capture and broke off the engagement. Sails were set and trimmed aboard the *Whydah*, to flee from the enemy and reach safety. But despite her sleek design and recent careening the *Whydah* was no faster or handier than the French frigate, and the two ships remained within sight of each other for the rest of the day. Only when night came on was Bellamy able to escape into the darkness.

Once again the *Whydah* needed to be taken to a safe anchorage to have the damage caused by the battle with the French repaired. The pirates set their course for Massachusetts. It was rumoured that Bellamy had a mistress at Cape Cod named Maria Hallett whom he wanted to visit, certainly the legends of the area say that was the case. Plagued by storms and constant damage to his ship, Bellamy was not destined to see Maria Hallet.

On the night of 26 April 1717 one of the most terrible storms the people of Massachusetts could remember blew up. The waves were 30-ft high and the strong winds were blowing off the sea towards the shore. Bellamy signalled his squadron to sail out to sea, away from the land, but they were already trapped within the treacherous shoals. Suddenly the stern of the *Whydah* was swept into a sandbar. The timbers creaked and crashed as they were broken asunder, the men at the helm lost steerage, and were powerless to prevent the next giant wave rolling the ship. Heavy cannon smashed through decks as the *Whydah* was rolled past the perpendicular, and the strained sounds of bending and snapping timber competed with the howl of the wind and waves as the ship broke apart. At last the *Whydah's* keel broke, and the whole ship separated, her contents spilled over the sea floor and her timbers were carried below the waves. 146 men were aboard the *Whydah* that night, and only two made it to the shore. Samuel Bellamy and the rest of the crew all perished.

At around the same time that Bellamy met his demise another name of note began to appear in the written record. A letter, dating from July 1717, but describing events of March 1717, is probably the first record of the pirate Edward Teach. Teach is better known now as the infamous Blackbeard, and it is quite likely that he came from Bristol[20]. It is difficult to tell exactly why Blackbeard is so well remembered today. Until his final battle there is no record of him ever having killed anyone, his career was not particularly long, or particularly successful when compared with some other pirates. Possibly we remember him now because of the tales about his fearsome appearance; Charles Johnson, for example, wrote in his *General History*:

> This beard was black, which he suffered to grow of an extravagant length; as to breadth it came up to his eyes. He was accustomed to twist it with ribbons, in small tails, after the manner of our Ramillies wigs, and turn them about his ears. In time of action he wore a sling over his shoulders with three brace of pistols hanging in holsters like bandoliers, and stuck lighted matches under his hat, which, appearing on each side of his face, his eyes naturally looking fierce and wild, made him altogether such a figure, that imagination cannot form an idea of a fury, from Hell, to look more frightful.

Probably we remember Blackbeard because he was so well known in his own time. His frightening, almost theatrical appearance, and the boldness of some of his exploits made him famous in his own lifetime, and his fame has never died.

Captain Johnson's *General History* tells us that Blackbeard served aboard privateers in the West Indies during the War of the Spanish Succession. Sometime, probably in 1716 Blackbeard became a pirate, and in late 1716 Captain Benjamin Hornigold appointed Blackbeard to his first command, probably a sloop of six guns. Blackbeard and Hornigold were among those pirates who made a base at New Providence (now Nassau) in the Bahamas. In 1717 a Royal proclamation was sent to New Providence, informing the pirates there that a large force of Royal Navy frigates was being dispatched, along with a new governor, to put an end to any pirates that did not submit to a Royal pardon within a certain date. The new governor, tasked with ending the pirate scourge in the West Indies was none other than Bristol sea dog Woodes Rogers.

As news of Rogers' imminent arrival spread amongst the pirates some of them decided to accept the pardon when it arrived, but many decided in favour of leaving the island and establishing themselves elsewhere. Blackbeard was amongst this number, and seems to have put to sea in the late summer of 1717.

Shortly afterwards Blackbeard fell in with another pirate, Stede Bonnet. It is probable that the two pirates sailed up the coast of North America in consort together for a while. By October Blackbeard had taken over Bonnet's ship, the *Revenge*, and Bonnet was reduced to supercargo, despite the fact that he had actually bought the *Revenge* and fitted her out at his own expense. Also in October Blackbeard captured several prizes, two of which, the *Sea-Nymph* and an unnamed sloop of twelve guns, were converted for the pirates' use. A little while later they exchanged the *Sea-Nymph* for another sloop and began to sail south, towards the Caribbean.

October 1717 was a busy and profitable month for the pirates. Apart from the prizes which were converted into pirate vessels, Blackbeard and his consorts captured a London ship belonging to Captain Cod, a trading vessel called a snow, two sloops from Madeira, one from London, and two from the West Indies. In the middle of the month Blackbeard met up once again with Hornigold and together they took eight barrels of sugar from a St Lucia sloop, then boarded and plundered a London ship. Four days later they plundered the *Robert* of Philadelphia and the *Good Intent* of Dublin.

In the middle of November Blackbeard, now with only two sloops, sighted and attacked a French slave ship, *La Concorde*. The French crew and 455 slaves were put ashore on the island of Bequia, near Grenada, and only 60 miles from their final destination. Blackbeard shifted his belongings and his flag to *La Concorde*, added extra cannon, and renamed her *Queen Anne's Revenge*. Within two weeks Blackbeard had increased the guns in the *Queen Anne's Revenge* from sixteen to thirty-two, and had begun to take larger prizes. Before the end of November the pirates took the *Great Allen* of Boston, sailing between Barbados and Jamaica. Captain Taylor of the *Great Allen* was 'very much abused', placed in irons and whipped for twenty-four hours until he revealed where the gold he was carrying had been hidden. The crew were then put ashore and the ship burned. A few days later the pirates took the *New Division*, a sloop of Antigua, but failed to lure the captain of another sloop aboard their ship. December 1717 and the early months of 1718 were spent cruising around the Caribbean and north Atlantic.

In May 1718 Blackbeard was reported in command of a sizeable force. He commanded the *Queen Anne's Revenge* himself, and was accompanied by Captain Richards, in command of the *Revenge*, and two other ships, one of which was probably commanded by Israel Hands; an estimated total force of 400 men. Around 22 May Blackbeard took his squadron to the mouth of Charlestown harbour, South Carolina, to take any vessel attempting to enter or leave. Within a few days they had captured the *Crowley*, commanded by Captain Clark, a small vessel from Charlestown and the *William* of Weymouth. Captain Richards of the *Revenge* was sent ashore with two hostages to negotiate with the Governor of Charlestown for a 'box of medicines'. If their terms were not met, the pirates threatened to slaughter their hostages, burn their prize ships, enter the harbour, burn the vessels there and finally destroy the town itself with gunfire. Historians have speculated and debated what sort of medicines or drugs could lead Blackbeard to blockade the busy harbour of a major American seaport. One theory that has been advanced is that Blackbeard's men were suffering from some sort of venereal disease and that the medicines were for that condition. Equally plausible is that the 'medicines' were laudanum, a drug with narcotic as well as medicinal uses. In any case the pirates were provided with their box of medicines and lifted their blockade.

The pirates looted whatever they could use from the ships they had captured, then released them and their crews. Sailing off to the northwards the pirates stole fourteen slaves from a Bristol ship, removed the cargo from a Boston ship and looted from a number of other prizes. Six days after Blackbeard's squadron left Charlestown they arrived off Topsail (now Beaufort) Inlet, North Carolina. The pirate ships had been at sea for some months and by now needed careening, so the *Queen Anne's Revenge* and three attendant sloops made to enter the inlet. At the entrance to the inlet however, Blackbeard ran the *Queen Anne's Revenge* aground. It has been generally supposed, even from the very time of its happening, that Blackbeard deliberately lost his ship to ensure a greater share of the spoils for himself and his favoured friends. Signals were made to the *Adventure*, commanded by Israel Hands, to come and tow Blackbeard's flagship off the sand bar, but instead the *Adventure* was also run aground. Blackbeard now transferred the treasure he had accumulated onto the *Revenge*, along with about forty of his comrades. The rest of the crews were left to starve or be captured, though it seems that most managed to escape.

Blackbeard then sailed for Bath Town, North Carolina where he enjoyed a good relationship with Governor Eden. By the end of June Blackbeard was at sea once more, sailing south towards Bermuda in the *Revenge* and another sloop. The pirates captured a number of English ships, plundering from them supplies and provisions that they required. Off Bermuda two French ships had the misfortune to fall in with Blackbeard. One was full of a cargo of sugar and cocoa, the other was empty. Teach placed all the French crew in the empty ship and returned to North Carolina with the now deserted, laden ship. At Bath Town Blackbeard claimed that he had found the ship adrift and empty and so, as the salver, was the rightful owner. A court upheld this claim and Blackbeard was able to remove the cargo legally. In case anyone should recognise the ship he had her condemned as leaky and burned at sea.

For four months Blackbeard and his crew remained in North Carolina, terrorising shipping and ravaging the land. Gangs of pirates roamed the countryside, taking what they required; food, drink, and women. Since the governor of North Carolina was a friend of the pirates the people could not seek help from him, and so it fell to the Governor of Virginia, Alexander Spotswood, to seek an end to the menace of Blackbeard.

Spotswood hired two small sloops and consulted with the captains of HMS *Lyme* and HMS *Pearl*, Royal Navy vessels based at Virginia. Volunteers from the Royal Navy ships manned the two sloops and the expedition was put under the command of Lieutenant Maynard of HMS *Pearl*. Maynard sailed on 17 November and arrived at the entrance to Ocracoke Inlet four days later. Blackbeard was entirely unprepared; some of his men were away ashore, many of those that remained were drunk. Maynard's sloops were unable to enter the inlet before night fell, so Blackbeard got his sloop ready for battle the next day, then sat down to an evening's drunkenness.

The following morning Maynard sent a boat ahead of the sloops to sound out the channel through the shoals. Suddenly a cloud of smoke and flame erupted from Blackbeard's sloop as the pirates fired a broadside. Maynard hoisted the Union flag and steered straight for Blackbeard's vessel. Blackbeard cut his anchor cable and set sail, continually firing his cannon at Maynard's sloop. The wind was not favourable for Maynard, so he had his men labour at the heavy oars to propel his sloop ever closer to Blackbeard's. Maynard had no cannon in either of his sloops so all they could do was receive the pirates' gunfire and respond with muskets when the distance became small enough.

Blackbeard stood upon his deck and drank a glass of strong spirit. He called out to Maynard that he would give no quarter, and Maynard called back that he expected none. As Maynard's two sloops came close to Blackbeard's the pirates fired a broadside of four guns loaded 'with all manner of small shot'. This wave of debris, probably consisting of all sorts of musket and pistol balls, broken glass, stones, bent nails and anything else the pirates could muster, swept across the decks of the two sloops. The men at the oars were virtually unprotected, the gunwale of the sloops being only about a foot above the deck. Twenty men were hit in Maynard's sloop, and nine in the other, including the midshipman in command. Maynard's second sloop could not recover and fell astern, but at this crucial moment a breath of wind blew up. Maynard ordered all of his men to hurry below deck where they would be much safer. Only the helmsman and Maynard himself kept the deck, and the helmsman was ordered to stay as low as possible beneath the gunwale.

As the two ships came together again Blackbeard's men threw grenades, 'filled with powder and small shot, slugs, and pieces of lead or iron'. The grenades had little effect since Maynard's men were mostly below deck. Blackbeard, seeing the deck of his enemy all but empty, assumed that most of Maynard's men had been killed or wounded. Blackbeard and fourteen of his men threw two more grenades onto the deck of Maynard's sloop then clambered from their ship to his under the cover of the smoke. When the smoke cleared Maynard gave the signal for his men, who climbed up from their place of safety and set about the pirates with cutlasses and pistols.

Blackbeard and Maynard sought each other out. Maynard fired his pistol at Blackbeard and wounded him. Blackbeard fired back but missed. Both men drew their swords, but under the rain of blows from Blackbeard's cutlass Maynard's blade snapped. Maynard stepped back and drew a second pistol, but before he could cock it Blackbeard was on him. Blackbeard lifted his sword to strike, Maynard feebly held out his arm to defend himself. Just as Blackbeard struck, one of Maynard's men slashed at his neck. Maynard received only a cut across his hand and was able to lift his pistol and fire it at close range into Blackbeard. It is said that Blackbeard received twenty-five wounds before he suddenly died, probably from the wound in his neck. Eight more of the pirates were killed, and the rest surrendered.

Maynard's second sloop rejoined the battle and boarded Blackbeard's sloop to attack the pirates left on board. One of Blackbeard's crew had been left orders to blow up the powder magazine of the sloop if it looked like it was going to be captured. Fortunately for Maynard's men a prisoner aboard the pirate sloop was able to prevent the man from carrying out his task. By the end of the action, ten of Maynard's fifty-five men had been killed and a further twenty-four were wounded. Blackbeard and nine of his crew were killed, and 'three white men and six negroes were taken alive but all much wounded'. Others of Blackbeard's crew were captured in the following days, and one of Maynard's wounded men died from his injuries.

Blackbeard's head was removed and fastened to the bowsprit of Maynard's sloop. The wounded seamen were treated and the two sloops set sail with their cargoes and prisoners for Virginia. The value of the prize goods taken from the pirate ships was divided among the crews of HMS *Lyme* and HMS *Pearl*. Governor Eden's secretary, who was accused of unlawful dealings with the pirates, died before he was questioned. Those members of Blackbeard's crew who were captured were tried and executed (except two, one of whom was acquitted, the other pardoned). What became of Blackbeard's head remains a mystery[21].

In the early days of 1721 a young Topsham man named John Phillips joined the crew of a ship bound for Newfoundland as a carpenter. On 19 April 1721 the ship was captured by the pirate Thomas Anstis, a Somerset man. Anstis had joined the pirate crew led by Howell Davis in 1718, and until the previous day had sailed in consort with Davis's successor, the notorious Bartholomew Roberts. It was common practice whenever pirates captured a ship to force any skilled men such as surgeons or carpenters to join their crew. If John Phillips had needed to be forced to join Anstis's crew he quickly reconciled himself to the life of a pirate, and remained the carpenter aboard Anstis's *Good Fortune* for over a year.

They took a number of good prizes, including a well armed ship which they put under the command of Anstis's gunner as a consort. The influx of new men into the pirate gang brought about factions and disagreement, and it was eventually decided to break the gang up. The difficulty lay in how to do so in such a way that everyone was satisfied, and at length it was agreed to sail together to a deserted island and petition for a pardon. The pirates waited on the island, but having heard no news of their pardon after nine months they once more fitted the *Good Fortune* and the consort *Morning Star* for sea, and set sail in August 1722. Shortly afterwards the *Morning Star* ran aground in the Cayman Islands, and as the *Good Fortune* stood into land to pick up the survivors two men-of-war came upon them.

Anstis's crew cut their cable and ran before the wind, leaving some of their comrades stranded at the mercy of the men-of-war. Only a lessening in the wind enabled the *Good Fortune* to escape by using her oars, with which the men-of-war were not equipped. Several more prizes were taken, including a frigate, which the pirates decided to convert to their own use. At the beginning of April 1723 the pirates reached Tobago where the frigate was emptied of her supplies in order to carry out the work necessary. While all the pirates were ashore HMS *Winchelsea* arrived at the island. The frigate was burned, Anstis and some of his men managed to make their escape in the *Good Fortune*, but the rest of the pirates fled into the hinterland of the island. Anstis was later murdered in his sleep, but Phillips was one of those who remained on Tobago. After a short while those pirates left on Tobago were able to capture a sloop and, tiring of piracy, sailed for England.

The sloop reached England in October 1723. The pirates sunk the sloop in the Bristol Channel and went ashore, posing as innocent civilians. The ruse was unsuccessful, for after the gang split up several of them were arrested and taken to Bristol jail. News of this reached Phillips, who was visiting his old friends in Devon, and he decided to flee England aboard a Topsham ship, bound for Newfoundland. Phillips never intended to make the return journey, and determined on a life of piracy. Charles Johnson, in his *General History*, explained why Newfoundland was such a fertile ground for the recruitment of pirates:

> Our West Country fishing ships, viz. from Topsham, Barnstaple and Bristol who chiefly attend the fishing seasons, transport over a considerable number of poor fellows every summer, whom they engage at low wages, and are by their terms to pay for passage back to England ... The masters residing there think advantages taken on their necessities [i.e. substantial profits made on essential provisions], no more than a just and lawful gain; and either bind such for the next summer's service, or sell their provisions out to them at extravagant rates; ... wherefore not being able to subsist themselves, or in any likely way of clearing the reckoning to their masters, they sometimes run away with shallops and boats, and begin on piratical exploits.

It was exactly those problems facing the Newfoundland workers that Phillips counted on when he took employment in a fish-curing factory. He gathered sixteen other like minded men together and they planned to steal a ship from Peter Harbour, and set off on the piratical account. When the day came, 29 August, only five men, including Phillips, kept the rendezvous. Nevertheless they agreed to carry out their plan and during the night stole a small vessel and put to sea. Phillips was appointed captain, John Nutt was made the sailing master, James Sparks was the gunner, Thomas Fern was the carpenter. According to the articles they drew up (reprinted in the Appendix) Phillips was to receive a share and a half as captain, the others to receive a share and a quarter as other officers. Only William White was to receive a single share, being the only 'private man' aboard.

Among the fishing fleet of Newfoundland Phillips was able to take a number of prizes, from which they were able to take provisions, and perhaps more importantly, recruits. One of the recruits taken from a fishing vessel was a sea dog called John Rose Archer, who had sailed with Blackbeard years before. Because of his experience Archer was promoted to quartermaster of the ship, now called *Revenge*.

At around the beginning of October 1723 Phillips and the *Revenge* arrived off Barbados and began to hunt for prizes. For three months they failed to sight a single ship, during which time their provisions grew shorter and shorter. When they finally did come across a French merchantman from Martinique she was far too large and well armed for them to capture her by force. The starving pirates, though, were desperate. They hoisted their colours, a black flag with a skeleton holding a spear and an hourglass, and demanded that the Frenchmen surrender, or they would receive no quarter. Incredibly the Frenchmen surrendered at once, and the crew of the *Revenge* were able to fill their hold with fresh supplies. Thus fortified they went on to capture a merchant sloop and a privateer in the following few days.

In the first weeks of 1724 the pirates took a trading vessel of the type called a snow, and a prize crew of four was put into her, under the command of Fern the carpenter. Fern had been outraged when Archer was promoted above him, and now he persuaded his comrades to sail off with the prize, leaving Phillips behind. As soon as the men aboard the *Revenge* realised what Fern was doing they began to chase, and soon caught the prize up. There was a brief skirmish in which one of the conspirators was killed and another wounded in the leg. Without a surgeon aboard it fell to Fern, as carpenter, to amputate the leg, which he did with 'the biggest saw'.

A little while later, having taken more prizes, Fern once again tried to make off with one of the ships, but on this occasion Phillips killed him. A few days later another man tried the same thing, and met the same fate. In March the pirates took two Virginia ships, one commanded by a John Phillips, the other by a Captain Mortimer. While Phillips was aboard Mortimer's ship the *Revenge's* boat came alongside and one of the men in it called to Phillips that a mutiny had broken out on his ship. Captain Mortimer seized his opportunity, and clubbed Phillips over the head. The wound did not render Phillips unconscious, and the pirate retaliated with his sword. Soon two of Phillips' men joined in the fray and Captain Mortimer was 'presently cut to pieces'. Two of Mortimer's own men apparently stood by and offered their captain no assistance.

This cruelty and intolerance Phillips displayed served on the one hand to bring his band more under his control, but on the other hand to stiffen the resolve of those opposed to him. Among the crew of the *Revenge* by now were a large number of men forced to join the pirates, in fact they probably outnumbered those who had joined voluntarily. Two of these forced men, Edward Cheeseman and John Philmore began to plot between themselves, and soon had a number of other sympathetic forced men.

In the first two weeks of April, Phillips captured at least thirteen ships. One of them was a schooner owned by the same man as had originally owned the *Revenge* before Phillips stole it. When he heard this Phillips ordered the schooner to be set free unharmed. The master of another forced the pirates to chase him for most of the day, so when they finally captured the ship in the evening they forced the master to dance around the deck until he was too weak to continue. On 14 April Phillips captured a ship, the master of which was one Andrew Harradine, whom the pirates forced aboard their own ship.

Harradine joined the conspiracy led by Cheeseman and Philmore, and on 18 April they put their plan into action. Cheeseman was working on the deck. Also on the deck were Harradine, Philmore, Burril the boatswain, John Nutt, and possibly one or two others.

After passing a Brandy bottle around Cheeseman began a conversation about the weather with John Nutt, while Philmore picked up Cheeseman's axe. At Harradine's wink Cheeseman heaved Nutt over the side of the ship, while Philmore split Burril's head with the axe. Nutt had hold of Cheeseman's sleeve, but by punching his arm Cheeseman forced him to let go.

The noise of all this action brought Phillips and some others up on to the deck. Cheeseman hit Phillips in the face with a mallet, breaking his jaw. Phillips again took a blow to the head without falling, and Harradine now approached him with Cheeseman's adze. James Sparks, the gunner, stepped in front of Phillips to protect him, but Cheeseman managed to trip him. Sparks fell into the grasp of another conspirator named Ivymay, who threw him over the side after Nutt. Harradine set about Phillips with the adze, while Cheeseman leapt into the hold and set about John Rose Archer with his mallet.

Cheeseman would have killed Archer had a young lad not suggested that Archer should be spared so that he could testify to the innocence of the forced men. William White, the only original member of Phillips' crew left alive, was also taken prisoner, along with two or three other pirates. The conspirators changed their course and put in at Boston. All aboard the Revenge were tried, but the conspirators against Phillips were all acquitted. Cheeseman was rewarded with the post of carpenter aboard HMS *Kinsale*. Archer and White were hanged on 2 June 1724, repenting their sins, begging forgiveness, and warning others not to follow in their ways.

Very few did follow in the ways of Archer and White. Although piracy continued, and indeed still continues today, the true Golden Age of piracy ended in the mid-1720s. Pirates still plied the oceans, but never again would such a concentration of them exist in one place at the same time as had existed in the Atlantic between 1715 and 1725. More wars broke out with Spain and France, in 1726

10,000 more seamen were employed in the Royal Navy than had been in 1725, and the number of privateers must have been similarly increased. Over the following century the Royal Navy proved that Britannia ruled the waves, in fact if not in theory, and the men of the West Country played as great a part in England's final naval superiority as they had always played in piratical and legitimate defence of the nation.

APPENDIX I

WESTERN MEN IN PIRATE CREWS

It has been estimated that around thirty-five per cent of pirates operating during the early eighteenth century were of English origin, and more than a few were West Country men. Naturally only a small proportion of these men rose to become captains, so their stories are never told and their names forgotten. The records of mass trials of pirate crews often shed a certain amount of light on the composition of pirate crews, and frequently towns in the West Country are mentioned as places of birth, or as places from which the pirates sailed before they turned to piracy. Here, then, are some relevant extracts from lists recording the crews of John Quelch, Charles Harris, and Bartholomew Roberts.

The Trial of John Quelch and others of his Company, held at Boston, June 13 1704.

(John Quelch had led a mutiny aboard the privateer *Charles*. Under his command the mutineers turned pirate and spent several months attacking Portuguese shipping in the South Atlantic. They were captured and tried at Boston. Six of the pirates were executed, the rest escaped punishment.)

The twenty-five numbered names listed among the crew of the *Charles* include the following:

4. Christoph. Scudamore, A cooper, served his Time at Bristol in England, Aged about 28 years (executed)
8. John Dorothy, Blacksmith, Born at Bristol in England, Aged about 25 years.
9. John Pitman, Sailor, Born at Bristol in England, Aged about 27 years
10. Charles King, Sailor, Born at Bristol in England, Aged about 19 years
18. Charles James, Mariner, Born in Gloucestershire in England, Aged about 54 years

The Tryals of the Pirates Taken by His Majesty's Ship the Swallow, Begun at Cape Coast Castle on the Coast of Africa, March the 28ᵗʰ 1722

(Bartholomew Roberts was one of the most notorious pirates of the golden age. In a career lasting nearly four years he is believed to have taken around 400 prizes. He built up a large, powerful squadron but was hunted down and killed in battle with HMS *Swallow* on the African coast. The executions which followed the trial of the captured pirates was the largest mass hanging of pirates in the eighteenth century.)

Of the fifty-two pirates executed at Cape Coast the following were
West Country men.

William Magnes, 35, Minehead

William Williams, 40, near Plymouth

Daniel Harding, 26, Croomsbury in Somersetshire

William Fernon, 22, Somersteshire

Jo. More, 19, Meer in Wiltshire

Abraham Harper, 23, Bristol

Jo. Parker, 22, Winifred in Dorsetshire (taken from the *Willing Mind*
   of Poole)

Peter Scudamore, 35, Bristol (taken from the *Mercy Galley* of
   Bristol)

John Walden, 24, Somersetshire

Israel Hynde, 30, Bristol (taken from the *Mercy Galley* of Bristol)

Charles Bunce, 26, Exeter

Robert Birtson, 30, Other St Maries, Devonshire

Richard Harris, 45, Cornwall (taken from the *Phoenix* of Bristol)

Joseph Nositer, 26, Sadbury in Devonshire (taken from the
   Expedition of Topsham)

Benjamin Jeffreys, 21, Bristol

Cuthbert Goss, 21, Topsham (taken from the *Mercy Galley* of
   Bristol)

John Jessup, 20, Plymouth

Thomas Giles, 26, Minehead. (taken from the *Mercy Galley* of
   Bristol)

Not all of the pirates were executed, some were acquitted, and
twenty were able to have their sentences reduced to servitude in
the Royal Africa Company, including:

Roger Scot, of the City of Bristol

Thomas How of Barnstaple, in the County of Devon

David Littlejohn of Bristol (taken from the *Phoenix* of Bristol)

Henry Dennis of Bideford

Hugh Harris of Corfe Castle, Devonshire (taken from the *Willing Mind* of Poole)

William Taylor of Bristol (taken from the *York* of Bristol)

Thomas Owen of Bristol

David Rice of Bristol

In addition the following pirates were taken from West Country ships by Roberts and joined his crew.

Thomas Wills (taken from the *Richard* of Bideford)

William Mackintosh (taken from the *Richard* of Bideford)

William Child (taken from the *Mercy Galley* of Bristol)

John Griffin (taken from the *Mercy Galley* of Bristol)

The Trial of Charles Harris and his crew, Rhode Island, July 10 1723.

(Charles Harris was a consort of both George Lowther and Ned Low. His ship was captured in June 1723 when Low deserted him to his fate.)

Of the thirty-five members of Harris's crew captured only four were Western men.

Peter Kneeves, 32, Exeter in Devon

Abraham Lacy, 21, Devonshire

John Tompkins, 23, Gloucestershire

John Waters, quartermaster, 35, County of Devon.

All four were executed 19 July 1723

APPENDIX II

BALLADS OF WESTERN PIRATES

All three of these ballads were written and printed a short time after the events they describe. The first two ballads, dealing with Henry Avery of Plymouth, were probably penned no later than 1700. The third ballad, the story of Blackbeard, was printed in 1719 and has been attributed to a young Benjamin Franklin. The details in the ballad suggest that its author consulted newspaper accounts of Blackbeard's last fight:

Villany Rewarded; or, The Pirate's Last Farewell to the World.

Who was executed at Execution Dock on Wednesday, the 25th of November, 1696, being of Every's crew; together with their Free Confession of their most Horrid Crimes.

Well may the world against us cry; for these our deeds most base,
For which alas! We now must die, death looks us in the face,
Which is no more than what's our due, since we so wicked were,
As here shall be declar'd to you. Let pirates then take care.

We with our comrades, not yet ta'en, together did agree,
And stole a ship out of the Groyne, to roam upon the sea;
With which we robb'd and plundered too, no ship that we did spare.
Thus many a one we did undo. Let pirates then take care.

Our ship being well stored then for this enterprise,
One hundred and men there was in her likewise:
We pillag'd all we could come nigh, no nation did we spare,
For which a shameful death we die. Let pirates then take care.

We robb'd a ship upon the seas, the Gunsway[22] call'd by name,
Which we met near the East Indies, and rifled the same;
In it was gold and silver store, of which all had a share;
Each man 600 pounds and more. Let pirates then take care.

Thus for some time we liv'd and reign'd as master of the sea;
Every merchant we detained and us'd most cruelly.
The treasures took, we sunk the ship, and those that in it were
That would not unto us submit. Let pirates then take care.

Thus wickedly we every day liv'd upon others' good,
The which, alas! we must repay now with our dearest blood;
For we on no one mercy took, nor any did we spare.
How can we then for mercy look? Let pirates then take care.

We thus did live most cruelly, and of no danger thought,
But we at last, as you may see, are unto justice brought

For outrages of villainy, of which we guilty are,
And now this very day must die. Let pirates then take care.

Now farewell to this wicked world, and our companions too;
From hence we quickly shall be hurl'd to clear the way for you;
For certainly if e're you come to justice, as we are,
Deserved death will be your doom. Then pirates all take care.

A Copy of Verses Composed by Captain Henry Every, Lately Gone to Sea to Seek His Fortune

Come all you brave boys whose courage is bold,
Will you venture with me? I'll glut you with gold.
Make haste unto Corunna; a ship you will find
That's called the Fancy, will pleasure your mind.

Captain Every is in her and calls her his own;
He will box her about, boys, before he has done.
French, Spaniard and Portuguese, the heathen likewise,
He has made a war with them until that he dies.

Moulded like wax work and she sails like the wind;
She is rigged and fitted and curiously trimmed,
And all things convenient has for his design.
God bless his poor Fancy, she's bound for the Main.

Farewell, fair Plymouth, and Cat-down be damned;
I once was part-owner of most of that land,
But as I am disowned so I'll abdicate
My person from England to attend on my fate.

Then away from this climate and temperate zone
To one that's more torrid you'll hear I am gone,
With a hundred and fifty brave sparks of this age
Who are fully resolved their foes to engage.

These northern parts are not fitting for me.
I'll raise the Antherhise, and some men shall see;
I am not afraid to let the world know
That to the South Seas and to Persia I'll go.

Our names shall be blazed and spread in the sky,
And many brave places I hope to descry,
Where never a French man e'er yet has been,
Nor any proud Dutchman can say he has seen.

My commission is large, and I made it myself,
And the capstan shall stretch it full larger by half;
It was dated in Corunna, believe it, my friend,
From the year ninety-three unto the world's end.

I honour St. George, and his colours I wear;
Good quarters I give, but no nation I spare.
The world must assist me with what I do want:
I'll give them my bill when my money is scant.

Now this I do say and solemnly swear,
He that strikes to St. George the better shall fare;
But he that refuses shall suddenly spy,
Strange colours aboard of my Fancy to fly.

Four chivileges of gold in a bloody field
Environed with green, now this is my shield;

Yet call out for quarters before you do see
A bloody flag out, which is our decree.

No quarters to give, no quarters to take.
We save nothing living, alas 'tis too late:
For we are now sworn by the bread and the wine,
More serious we are than any divine.

Now this is the course I intend for to steer.
My false-hearted nation, to you I declare
I have done thee no wrong: thou must me forgive.
The world shall maintain me as long as I live.

The Downfall of Piracy

Being a full and true account of a desperate and bloody sea-fight
between Lieutenant Maynard and that noted pirate Captain Teach,
commonly call'd by the name of Black-beard; Maynard had fifty
men, thirty-five of which were kill'd and wounded in the action;
Teach had twenty-one, most of which was kill'd and the rest carried to Virginia in order to take their Tryal.

Will you hear of a bloody battle, lately fought upon the seas?
It will make your ears to rattle and your admiration cease:
Have you heard of Teach the rover, and his knavery on the main;
How of gold he was a love, how he loved ill-got gain?

When the act of grace appeared Captain Teach and all his men
Unto Carolina steered, where they us'd him kindly then;
There he marry'd to a lady, and gave her five hundred pound,
But to her he prov'd unsteady, for he soon marched off the ground

And returned, as I tell you, to his robberies as before:
Burning, sinking ships of value, filling them with purple gore.
When he was at Carolina, there the Governor did send
To the Governor of Virgina, that he might assistance lend.

Then the man-of-war's commander, two small sloops he fitted out;
Fifty men he put on board sir, who resolved to stand it out.
The lieutnant he commanded both the sloops and you shall hear
How before he landed he suppress'd them without fear

Valiant Maynard as he sailed soon the pirate did espy;
With his trumpet he then hailed, and to him they did reply:
'Captain Teach is our commander', Maynard said 'He is the man
Whom I am resolved to hang sir, let him do the best he can.'

Teach replied unto Maynard, 'You no quarter here shall see
But be hanged on the main-yard, you and all your company.'
Maynard said 'I none desire of such knaves as thee and thine.'
'None I'll give,' Teach then replied; 'my boys, give me a glass of wine.'

He took the glass and drank damnation unto Maynard and his crew,
To himself and generation, then the glass away he threw.
Brave Maynard was resolv'd to have him, tho' he'd cannons nine or ten;
Teach a broadside quickly gave him, killing sixteen valiant men.

Maynard boarded him and to it they fell with sword and pistol too;
They had courage, and did show it, killing of the pirate's crew.
Teach and Maynard on the quarter fought it out most manfully;
Maynard;s sword did cut him shorter, losing his head he there did die.

Every sailor fought while he, sir, power had to wield his sword,

Not a coward could you see, sir, fear was driven from aboard;
Wounded men on both sides fell, sir, 'twas a doleful sight to see,
Nothing could their courage quell, sir; O they fought courageously.

When the bloody fight was over we're informed by a letter writ,
Teach's head was made a cover to the jack-staff of the ship;
Thus they sailed to Virginia and when they the story told
How they killed the pirates many, they'd applause from young and old.

APPENDIX III

ARTICLES ABOARD THE *REVENGE*

It was common practice aboard pirate ships in the late seventeenth and eighteenth centuries to draw up a list of rules, known as 'Articles' which each member of the crew was obliged to sign and adhere to. Although mentions of articles or 'signing articles' are common in period documents we only have the texts of a handful of sets surviving to us today. One of the sets of articles recorded in Charles Johnson's *General History* is that of John Phillips' crew aboard the *Revenge*.

1. Every Man shall obey civil Command; the Captain shall have one full Share and a half in all Prizes; the Master, Carpenter, Boatswain and Gunner shall have one Share and a quarter.
2. If any Man shall offer to run away, or keep any Secret from the Company, he shall be marroon'd with one Bottle of Powder, one Bottle of Water, one small Arm, and Shot.

3. If any Man shall steal any Thing in the Company, or game, to the Value of a Piece of Eight, he shall be Marroon'd or Shot.

4. If at any Time we should meet another Marrooner (that is, Pyrate,) that Man shall sign his Articles without the consent of our Company, shall suffer such Punishment as the Captain and Company shall think fit.

5. That Man that shall strike another while these Articles are in force, shall receive Moses's Law (that is 40 Stripes lacking one) on the bare Back.

6. That Man that shall snap his Arms, or smoak Tobacco in the Hold, without a cap to his Pipe, or carry a Candle lighted without a Lanthorn, shall suffer the same Punishment as in the former Article.

7. That Man that shall not keep his Arms clean, fit for an Engagement, or neglect his Business, shall be cut off from his Share, and suffer such other Punishment as the Captain and the Company shall think fit.

8. If any Man shall lose a Joint in time of an Engagement, shall have 400 Pieces of Eight; if a limb, 800.

9. If at any time you meet with a prudent Woman, that Man that offers to meddle with her, without her Consent, shall suffer present Death.

END NOTES

1 On one occasion, for example, seamen from Fowey attacked a squadron of ships from the Cinque Ports

2 The story of the famous lady-pirate, Lady Killigrew, is to be found in several books and other works, but important details are almost always absent or conflicting between reports. It is difficult, for example, for the casual reader to ascertain for sure which Lady Killigrew was the famous lady-pirate, her relationship to the head of the household of the time, the nationality of the ship she supposedly plundered, and even when the supposed piracy took place. I believe that the incident which follows provided the basis for the tale of the famous lady-pirate Killigrew, for many of the principal elements are the same – the rumours of gold hidden in a ship forced into Falmouth by bad weather etc. If this is indeed the case then a number of unresolved points can be resolved. The attack took place

in 1582 against a Spanish ship with a number of Flemish crew men, and the Lady Killigrew who played the largest part was Elizabeth, mother of the Sir John who held the title at that time. Important to note is that Lady Killigrew did not actually take part in the boarding herself as she is often purported to have done. I believe this to have been a mistake on the part of some past historian who misunderstood the phrase 'leading spirit', which was used to describe Lady Killigrew's part in the exploit. The same mistake was repeated over and over until it became an accepted fact that Lady Killigrew was a 'lady-pirate'. This was not the case. Subsequent researchers have looked in vain for evidence of Lady Killigrew personally involving herself in a boarding and their lack of success has possibly led to the confusion over the details of the issue.

3 Although Spain was considered an 'unfriendly power' in Elizabethan England it was not until the Treaty of Nonsuch of 1585 that the two countries formally went to war. Before that date all the attacks by English sea dogs on Spain and her empire must be considered acts of piracy, but after that date it is more proper to think of them as acts of patriotism. While it is tempting to include some of the privateering exploits of West Country men like John Chudley and others I feel that they really lie outside the scope of this book, and several works are readily available which cover that subject. 'The Sea Dogs' by Neville Williams, for example, is a readable yet scholarly work.

4 Drake's circumnavigation is without question the best known exploit of any individual Tudor sea dog, and is second only to the defeat of the Spanish Armada in 1588 in terms of incidents best remembered from that period. As such, the history of Drake's circumnavigation is well recorded in numerous books, magazines, television programs, websites and other media, often in great detail. Consequently, although it must be considered the crowning moment of Drake's piratical career, and the greatest achievement of any West Country pirate, I have decided to keep my narrative of the voyage as brief as is reasonable. Readers interested in Drake's

circumnavigation are urged to read the anonymous first hand account of the voyage contained in Richard Hakluyt's *Principal Voyages* and reprinted in numerous anthologies, or to consult the excellent biography *Sir Francis Drake*, by George Malcolm Thomson.

5 The North-West passage was the sea route into the Pacific around the north of Canada which was assumed to exist. During the Elizabethan period the arctic explorers Martin Frobisher and John Davis both mounted expeditions in search of the passage from the Atlantic end, without success. Davis was on the right course but was forced to turn back by lack of supplies and the will of his crew. Despite several other attempts in the following centuries by men such as 'North-West' Foxe and Captain Franklin, it was not until 1905 that Roald Amundsen became the first man to succeed at the passage.

6 There is some question whether it was the same renegade Murat Reis that carried out both the Iceland and Baltimore attacks. It has been suggested that there were two European renegades using the same name at the same time, one German and one Flemish. Since Murat Reis was the name of a famous sixteenth-century corsair it is possible that the name was a popular one to adopt, but the likelihood is that both raids were in fact the work of one pirate. An English merchant sent to redeem English captives in 1646 paid an average price of £38 per slave, but the price of young female captives was considerably higher. One Irish woman cost £1,392. To put that in perspective, the captain of a first rate man of war in the Royal Navy in 1646 was paid £14 per month, or £182 per year. Murat Reis captured between 400 and 800 slaves on his Iceland raid. Taken at the lowest estimate, and assuming each slave to have been worth only £38 still meant an approximate haul of £15,200, over ninety year's wages for a first rate Royal Navy captain.

7 This may have been, but was probably not, the same George Estcourt, alias Willis, who received a pardon for piracy on 27 February 1605.

8 Reports exist from this time of Easton commanding a fleet of forty
   ships, a number that has been repeated by subsequent historians.
   As we have seen he probably commanded no more than thirteen
   or fifteen vessels while in English waters, and the report of forty is
   clearly an alarmist exaggeration. In 1611 the Royal Navy of England
   had only thirty ships, so even a force of a dozen or so was a serious
   threat. The size of ships should also be taken into account. Easton's
   ship the *Fortune* was 160 tons and mounted twenty-two guns, a very
   similar size to HMS *Tramontana*. The *Concord*, Easton's flagship in
   1611 was 240 tons, and probably carried somewhere in the region
   of thirty guns. At that time one third of the Royal Navy's warships
   were smaller than Easton's.

9 This sentiment of Easton's is attributed to John Ward in the
   contemporary ballad *Ward the Pirate*, which concludes "Go home, go
   home,' says Captain Ward, 'And tell your King for me, 'If he reigns
   King on all the land Ward will reign King on the sea'. The story
   may be apocryphal in either case, but it was certainly attributed to
   Easton before Ward.

10 A certain amount of confusion is caused by John Nutt's early
   career, and his becoming a pirate. A century later, in 1723, another
   West Country man named John Phillips, whom we shall meet in
   a later chapter, sailed in a Topsham vessel to Newfoundland where
   he jumped ship and gathered about him a band of ruffians to go
   to sea as pirates. The navigator of this band was called John Nutt.
   Because of the number of similar elements to the story – Topsham,
   Newfoundland, the gathering of a crew, and of course the name
   – the deeds of these two John Nutts are often confused by lazy
   researchers.

11 Very little information is available about the Barbary pirates who
   joined forces with Nutt, except that they had a considerable
   force. It is tempting to suppose that their commander may have
   been the notorious renegade Murat Reis. There were very few
   Barbary pirates at that time with such a large squadron under their

command, and it was only a year previously that Murat, or Jan
Janszoon, had carried out his legendary raid on Baltimore, not far
from Nutt's base at Crookhaven. However, Murat Reis's activities
after the Baltimore raid until nearly a decade later are more or less
unknown, so it is impossible to be certain one way or the other.

12   Browne Bushell, the man in question is one of the most interesting
and enigmatic figures of the civil war. He was neither from the
West Country, nor did he operate from the area, so his story would
be out of place in this book. Nevertheless, the fact that he was
captured by Parliament at Weymouth gives me an excuse to include
the briefest of biographies here. Bushell began the war as a naval
officer on the side of Parliament, but the arrival of the Queen
in his native Yorkshire convinced him and his cousin Sir Hugh
Cholmondley to join the Royalists. However, Sir Hugh had some
goods at Hull that he wanted to secure before they were confiscated
to Bushell was sent to retrieve them. While in Hull Bushell was
captured and agreed to aid the Parliamentarians. Some time later,
while left in command of Scarborough Castle Bushell declared his
new allegiance to Parliament. Within months Bushell was once
again corresponding with the Royalists, and soon handed the castle
over to them, before taking to sea as a Royalist privateer. After a
successful time plundering ships in the North Sea and the Channel
Bushell was captured off Weymouth in 1645, but turned coat again
and was soon in command of a Parliamentarian privateer. In 1648
a large part of the fleet mutinied and carried their ships to join the
Royalists, and Bushell too declared for the King once more. He was
quickly captured and offered to join the Parliamentarians again, but
his offer was refused and in March 1651 he was hanged as a pirate.
It may seem strange that Bushell was able to change sides so many
times but in civil war there is always a shortage of skilled artificers
such as seamen, engineers and gunners, so it was not uncommon
for those sorts of men to be well treated when they were captured.
Bushell was just too perfidious.

13 There were ten *Whelps* built in 1628. Two of them were employed
by Plumleigh against Robert Nutt in 1632, and indeed their
principal function was to hunt down pirates and privateers whose
fast frigates could outsail most ships then in the English Navy. By
1643 two of the *Whelps* had been hulked, one sold, one given away,
and four lost at sea. Only the Eighth and Tenth remained in service.

14 Captain Nathaniel Butler, cribbing from Sir Henry Mainwaring
(both of them pirates of a sort at times), described a weft. 'This
word weft, when it is a noun, intimateth such signs or shows as
from aboard ships are made to boats or men when they would have
them to come aboard them hastily from the shore or elsewhere;
and these wefts are commonly some sea coats, or gowns, or the like,
heaved (that is waved) abroad or hung out upon the shrouds of the
ship. But whensoever any of these shows are hung out by a ship,
being at sea, it is received as a signal that she is in some imminent
peril'. It is probably fair to assume that in this case the persons taken
aboard were enticed so by the former kind of weft.

15 The story of the men who remained in the Pacific under
Bartholomew Sharpe is an interesting one, but too long and
irrelevant to reproduce here. One account of the voyage was
written by Basil Ringrose and can be found fairly easily, included
in later editions of Exquemeling's *Buccaneers of America*. *Brethren of
the Coast* by Peter Kemp and Christopher Lloyd includes one of
the best accounts of the expedition written in recent years. Various
other accounts, including that of Sharpe himself are available, but are
somewhat harder to find.

16 Dampier's voyage in the *Roebuck* can hardly be called piratical so
has no place in this book, but a brief outline may be of interest
to the reader, and ought perhaps to be included for the sake of
completeness. The *Roebuck* sailed in January 1699 with provisions
for twenty months. Calling briefly at the Canaries, and the Cape
Verde Islands, Dampier then made his way round the Cape of Good
Hope and touched the west coast of Australia in July. He explored

the coastline around the latitude of 26° S, but found no useable harbour and no sign of fresh water or provisions. In September Dampier sailed from Australia to Timor, and thence to New Guinea, arriving at the beginning of December. He began to survey the northern parts of New Guinea, but his deficiencies as a leader led to discontent among his men and he was forced to break off his exploration to avoid mutiny. Towards the end of 1700 the *Roebuck* passed the Cape of Good Hope for the second time and entered the Atlantic Ocean. In February 1701 his leaky ship foundered off Ascension Island and Dampier was forced to put himself and his crew ashore. In April a convoy of East India Company vessels rescued the marooned men.

17 The identity of Captain Charles Johnson is a mystery. Since the 1930s it has been suggested that Johnson was a pseudonym for Daniel Defoe, and so compelling are the arguments, on the face of it, that several major libraries re-catalogued the *General History*, and many authors still write of 'Defoe's *General History*…'. Without going into too many reasons too deeply it is in my opinion incredibly unlikely that Defoe wrote the *General History*. The writing styles are not particularly similar beyond certain similarities common to most writers of the early eighteenth century, there is just no good evidence that it was Defoe, and most importantly, Defoe and Nathaniel Mist (the publisher of the book) had fallen out dramatically years before the book's publication and never spoke to one another again. For a fuller explanation of the evidence surrounding Johnson's identity I would recommend Dr David Cordingly's introduction to the 1998 edition of the *General History*.

18 Although Captain Kidd set sail on his piratical voyage from Plymouth, his story is otherwise unconnected with the West Country, and so does not appear here, except in connection with that of Culliford. Several biographies of Kidd have been written, most recently Richard Zack's *The Pirate Hunter*, which is a very readable account.

19 There is some confusion about Condent's name. His surname is variously given as Condent, Condon, Congdon or some other similar form, but that can be put down to the inconsistency of eighteenth-century spelling. His forename is generally given in period sources as Edmund, but he has also been attributed with the forenames John, Christopher, and William. When Condent appears in modern histories he is usually called Christopher, but that is probably an error, repeated by subsequent researchers. I have settled on giving him the name Edmund Condent, as being the most likely forename and the most familiar spelling of his surname.

20 There is great debate among scholars about Blackbeard's identity. In period records his name is given variously as Teach, Titch, Thatch, Tiche, and Teague, and he also appears to have used the aliases Drummond and Kentish. Debate over Teach's birthplace is equally fierce. Historical records show that Teach was probably a mate on a Philadelphia sloop before he turned to piracy, and he may have had a brother in Jamaica. While both of these pieces of evidence offer tantalising possibilities of Blackbeard having been born in the New World neither of them rule out the possibility that he was born in Bristol. Captain Charles Johnson's chapter on Blackbeard opens with the sentence 'Edward Teach was a Bristol man born...', and while there is little evidence to prove that statement conclusively there is certainly none to disprove it.

21 There are at least two skulls purporting to be Blackbeard's, neither with any verifiable evidence in support of the claim.

22 An anglicised form of *Gang-I-Sawai*.

BIBLIOGRAPHY

Acts of the Privy Council 1574-78

Andriette, E.A., *Devon and Exeter in the Civil War* (David and Charles; Newton Abbot, 1971)

Burl, A., *Black Barty: Bartholomew Roberts and his Pirate Crew* (Alun Books; Port Talbot, 1997)

Butler, N., *Boteler's Dialogues* (Navy Records Society, 1920)

The Calendar of State Papers Domestic

The Calendar of State Papers Ireland

The Calendar of State Papers Venetian

Cooke, E., *A Voyage to the South Sea, and Round the World* (London, 1712)

Cordingly D., *Life Among the Pirates* (Little, Brown, and co.; London, 1995)

Dampier, W. *A New Voyage Round the World* (London, 1697)

Esquemeling, A.O., *The Buccaneers of America* (London, 1684)

Forster, J., *The Life of Sir John Eliot, vol.* 1 (London, 1865)

Hakluyt, R., *The Principal Navigations, Voyages, Traffiques and Discoveries of the English Nation, Made by Sea or Overland to the Remote and Farthest Distant Quarters of the Earth at any time within the compasse of these 1600 yeares* (London, 1589).

Johnson, C.*A General History of the Robberies and Murders of the Most Notorious Pirates, vols.* 1, 2 (London, 1724-28)

Kemp, P. and Lloyd, C., *Brethren of the Coast* (William Heinemann; London, 1960)

Manwaring, G.E. (ed.), *The Life and Works of Sir Henry Mainwaring, vols.* 1, 2 (Navy Records Society; 1920-22)

Mitchell, D., *Pirates* (Thames and Hudson; London, 1976)

Monson, W., *Naval Tracts, vols.* 3, 4, 5 (Navy Records Society; 1912-14)

Oppenheim, M.M., *The Maritime History of Devon* (University of Exeter Press; Exeter, 1968)

Rodger N.A.M., *Command of the Ocean* (Allen-Lane; London, 2004)

Rodger N.A.M., *Safeguard of the Seas* (Harper-Collins; London, 1997)

Rogers, W.*A Cruising Voyage Round the World* (London, 1712)

Souhami, D., *Selkirk's Island* (Orion; London, 2002)

Thompson, G.M., *Sir Francis Drake* (Secker and Warburg Ltd., 1972)

Williams, N., *The Sea Dogs: Privateers, Plunder and Piracy in the Elizabethan Age* (Macmillan; New York, 1975)

If you are interested in purchasing other books published by The History Press, or in case you have difficulty finding any of our books in your local bookshop, you can also place orders directly through our website

www.thehistorypress.co.uk